WHEN *Mary* FINDS US:

Finding Blackness in the Drama of Mary & The Seven Sayings of Mary

Alvin C. Bernstine and Diana Becton

Foreword
Reverend Dr. Jacqueline Thompson

ACB MINISTRIES

Copyright 2025 by Alvin C. Bernstine
Artistic Renderings by Yvonne Simmons

ISBN 979-8-9885340-2-0

Book design by Joyce Evans

Dedicated to the Black Church Mothers' Board and the spirit of Mother Rhoda Crosby
of the New Nazarene Missionary Baptist Church, Richmond, California,
and Nellie Dean Simmons of Third New Hope Baptist Church, Detroit, Michigan.

Black Church Mother's Boards humanize the church constructed by men.

ACKNOWLEDGEMENTS

[Alvin] I want to thank the three congregations that gave me both time and space to grow as a preacher: The Olivet Baptist Church of Nashville, Tennessee; the Mount Lebanon Baptist Church of Brooklyn, New York; and the Bethlehem Missionary Baptist Church of Richmond, California. These congregations did more than give me pulpits—they made me preach. Week after week, across forty years and three cities, your faithful presence compelled me to be creative, connected, provocative, prophetic, relevant, and celebratory.

Among all who shaped my preaching, none were more faithful than the Mothers' Boards. Those saintly matriarchs anchored my ministry in the common struggles of Black life, showing up until they no longer could. I am especially grateful to the Mothers' Board of Olivet Baptist Church, who recently invited me back to preach their Annual Day sermon (October 2024). That invitation reminded me that preaching must always reach across generations.

Finally, I must thank my incredible wife, Diana. With courage and grace, you joined me not only in preaching the Seven Sayings of Mary but also in grounding them theologically. You are my partner in ministry and in life. You are amazing, dear wife!

[Diana] Ever since I can remember, my mother and grandmother took me to church. They placed me on the pews before I could read a hymnbook, and they taught me, by their example, that faith was not something you talked about—it was something you lived.

I acknowledge with gratitude the faith communities that have shaped my journey. At Allen Temple Baptist Church, I was nurtured under the wise leadership of Rev. Dr. J. Alfred Smith, Sr. and strengthened by the mentorship of the Business and Professional Women of Allen Temple, who taught me what it means to be a woman of faith with purpose. Later, as a young mother, I carried my children into the welcoming arms of St. Augustine's Episcopal Church, where I encountered the beauty of worship that broadened my understanding of God's people. And for many years now, my spiritual home has been **Bethlehem Missionary Baptist Church**, where community, preaching, and a living witness to justice have grounded my faith and service.

This work would not exist without my beloved husband, Rev. Dr. Alvin C. Bernstine, who carried the vision for this project, did the heavy lifting in writing and research, and invited me into a collaboration that has stretched and blessed me in countless ways. His brilliance, his discipline, and his unwavering love are woven into every page of this book.

Finally, I give thanks to the countless women—mothers, grandmothers, aunties, church mothers, beauty shop theologians, and sisters in the struggle—whose voices, spoken and unspoken, fill the silences we seek to break here. This book belongs to them as much as it belongs to us.

Table of Contents

Foreword ix

An Eyewitness Testimony xi

Introduction: The Drama: Breaking the Silence of Mary in Black Church Life 1

Chapter 1: Hiding from Mary and the Virgin Birth: Black People's Issues with Sex 5

Chapter 2: Oh Mary, Don't You Weep 23

Chapter 3: Mariology Examined 33

Chapter 4: The Seven Sayings of Mary as Preached at Bethlehem Missionary Baptist Church, Richmond, California, Advent 2023 49

Chapter 5: The First Saying of Mary: Power of Divine Confusion........................ 51

Chapter 6: The Second Saying of Mary: From Confusion to Submission 57

Chapter 7: The Third Saying of Mary: Sister to Sister 63

Chapter 8: The Fourth Saying of Mary: Grown Folk's Music: When Christmas Grows Up 69

Chapter 9: The Fifth Saying of Mary: When Mary Finds Us................................ 75

Chapter 10: The Sixth Saying of Mary: A Heart for More in 2024 81

Chapter 11: The Seventh Saying of Mary (John 2:5) "What Mama Said".. 87

Chapter 12: A Sermonic Epilogue: The Testimony of A Great Finish................... 93

References.. 101

FOREWORD

Growing up in Oakland, and after only a few years in public school, my mother made a decision regarding my elementary school education. She took advantage of an opportunity to send me to a parochial school, a Catholic school specifically. I ended up attending Saint Louis Bertrand Elementary School and Holy Names High School. Every day, in class after pledging allegiance to the flag of the United States of America and reciting the Lord's Prayer - we hailed Mary. It was quite a controversial act for my Black Baptist parents who considered the veneration of Mary and prayer to Mary - idol worship. But after all these years, I still know that prayer by heart:

> Hail Mary, full of grace - the Lord is with thee,
> Blessed art thou among women and blessed is the fruit of thy womb Jesus
> Holy Mary, Mother of God pray for us sinners now and at hour of our death

This plea for intercession made across the world by millions, still finds rest in my heart. Perhaps it is because I now know what it feels like, after all these years, to desperately desire someone - anyone to entreat God to break the bonds of oppression that have plagued those of us relegated to the margins and treated as devoid of the "imago dei".

In an age when the voices of the marginalized are too often silenced, this work on Mariology stands as a clarion call to listen again — not just to the words spoken *about* Mary, but to the words spoken *by* her. This book, "WHEN MARY FINDS US: Finding Blackness in the Drama of Mary" brings together the prophetic utterances of the mother of Jesus and places them in conversation with the cries for freedom, justice, and wholeness that echo through the lives of Black people across generations.

Too often in theological discourse, Mary has been reduced to a passive vessel, her humanity overshadowed by piety, her prophetic voice lost beneath centuries of doctrinal polish. But here, the authors recover Mary's words — from her courageous "Be it unto me according to your word" to her radical "Do whatever he tells you" — lifting them up as sites of resistance, hope, and transformation for oppressed communities today.

This book is significant because it refuses to relegate Mary to the realm of sentimental devotion alone. Instead, it dares to read her sayings through the lens of Black Liberation Theology and Womanist thought, uncovering her solidarity with the poor, her defiance in the face of empire, her deep motherly lament, and her unwavering faith in a God who scatters the proud and lifts up the lowly. In Mary's words, we hear echoes of Sojourner Truth's defiant proclamations, Fannie Lou Hamer's righteous indignation, and the quiet prayers of grandmothers whose faith sustained entire generations.

The authors of this work are uniquely qualified to undertake this recovery. As husband-and-wife co-laborers—she a history making District Attorney and theologian, he a pastor-scholar—they embody the relational and intersectional tenets central to Womanist and Practical theology. Their shared ministry highlights how theology and praxis are lived in families, churches, courtrooms and pulpits alike. As scholars and pastors rooted in the Black Church tradition, they bring the rigor of theological scholarship alongside the lived wisdom of communities that know both the cross and the empty tomb. They write from the vantage point of those whose experiences of struggle and survival make Mary's sayings all the more resonant.

This book is a gift — not just to theologians and pastors, but to every person who longs for a faith that liberates, a faith that listens to women's voices, and a faith that recognizes that the God who came to us through Mary still comes to us through the cries, the prayers, and the songs of the oppressed.

May these pages invite you to hear Mary's seven sayings not as relics of the past, but as living words calling us to birth justice, embody hope, and trust, her words that declare that "with God, nothing shall be impossible."

Until Mary Finds Us,

Dr. Jacqueline A. Thompson, *Senior Pastor*
Allen Temple Baptist Church
Oakland, California
Second Vice-President
Progressive National Baptist Convention, Inc.

AN EYEWITNESS TESTIMONY

The human psyche is fascinating to me and is the reason I chose to study clinical psychology. An area I continue to explore is the impact of messaging on our perception of self, others, community, and the larger society. Messages are intentional to shape how we navigate the world. Theological messages hold another level of weightiness because we believe it is the word of God. This requires a special handling of how we interpret text. As a Black Woman Executive, Wife, and Mother I've consistently wrestled with messaging that liberates and messaging that imprisons. Once I became a Minster and then a Pastor my wrestling increased, at times, to a level of exhaustion. I believe this can lead some to burnout and others to just go with the flow. I'm thankful the manuscript you have in your hand fought against both.

As a lifelong member of Bethlehem Missionary Baptist Church, I had the privilege of sitting under two dynamic pastors. But it was the leadership of Pastor Alvin C. Bernstine that I began to question the theological frameworks that I'd been taught throughout childhood and my young adult years. I started to question the messaging. I never used my clinical training to wrestle with the biblical text or challenge the interpretations provided. Unconsciously, I learned this was a sacred area I was forbidden to explore. I say unconsciously because it wasn't explicitly stated but the messaging led me to believe there were those equipped for biblical exegesis and those who were the recipients of this gift.

Pastor Bernstine challenged that belief and opened a door leading to profound theological revelations that continue to unfold in my life today. He and First Lady Reverend Diana Becton's proclamation of *The Seven Sayings of Mary* during Advent 2023 was, yet, another pivotal theological experience. What I experienced was more than a sermon series—it was a revelation.

I've come to better understand the Jesus I love and serve as a liberating Christ. I've challenged the oppressive and marginalizing framing of my past and recognized how I was imprisoned by a Eurocentric white supremist framing of Christ that invisiblized my experience and kept me from an intimate relationship with Him. I want to be clear, this was intentional. Intentional messaging keeping me bound and held captive.

What I hadn't done was opened this liberated mindset to others in the biblical text. Here comes Pastor Bernstine and First Lady Reverend Diana Becton with a plot twist. They challenged the narrative of Mary as being, simply, a virgin who was used by God, to a girl who was more than her sexualized state.

The power of seeing Mary. Seeing her life as a life of courage and liberation. Seeing her life from a place I've navigated in my personal, professional, and spiritual life. Seeing myself in her as she was called to a place of confusion. Seeing the power of divine confusion renamed my experiences. Seeing her divine confusion leading her to submission but not the worldly understanding of submission that we push as a narrative for women. Seeing the submission opening a safe space for sister to sister greeting leading to worship in song. Mary's, "yes", wasn't a naïve girl just going with the flow. Mary's yes was an act of liberation shaping how we can see ourselves. Mary was no longer voiceless. She was courageous and fought against others attempt to narrate her life. How thankful I was to the profound privilege of having my theological world rocked.

As a daughter in ministry of Pastor Bernstine, I bear witness that his and Reverend Becton's preaching did not simply interpret Mary's sayings but embodied them. Their voices broke silences, challenged patriarchal limits, and invited our congregation into a new dialogue with God and with one another. We were led to challenge the theological messaging not only about Jesus but about all in the biblical text. More specifically, to understand how marginalization isn't confined to our current lived experiences but are present in the theological underpinning of how we view God's word.

The impact of this sermon series is still being discovered. I'm a witness to us being led to SEE Mary contributed to a historic moment in the life of our church: my election as the first woman pastor of Bethlehem Missionary Baptist Church. My call, ordination and subsequent election, affirmed by Bethlehem, was a living testimony that Mary's voice still creates space for women to lead, preach, and pastor at the highest level.

This manuscript captures not only the scholarship but the lived proclamation of those Advent Sundays. And I add my voice here as testimony: what you hold in your hands is not only theology—it is sacred memory, it is witness, it is the living Word that found us at Bethlehem and continues to guide me and our congregation into new possibilities.

Dr. Carolyn Mckinley-Alvarez, Psy.D.
Senior Pastor of Bethlehem Missionary Baptist Church
Richmond, California

"Where Dem Chirren At?"

(Poetic refrains on When Mary Finds Us from a Black mother's worried heart.)

Porch light cuttin' through the city dark,
This rocker creakin' out a question mark—
Baby, where you walkin' in this night so deep?
Ain't no peace where stray souls sleep.

I hear sirens whisperin' where prayers used to be,
Ain't no choir hummin'—just the cold, free
Wind chasin' dreams down these asphalt streets,
While my heart counts time to your missin' beats.

Why you wander, child? Don't you know the cost?
Ain't no truth in glitter—just love that's lost.
Granny's words hang like smoke in the air,
Who gon' hold you when the world don't care?

But Mary's out there searchin' with my same tired eyes,
Callin' all our babies back under heavy skies.
She knows the ache that keeps a mother up at night—
Tryna turn lost boys back towards the light.
So come home, baby. Let the porch light lead.
There's grace in biscuits—love in every seed.
You ain't too far gone—you just forgot your name.
Mary knows the way. Child, just leave the shame.

The table's set. The door's on the latch.
Come on home. It ain't too late to match
Your breath with mine beneath this same old moon—
A mother's prayer ain't never sung out of tune.

Mary still asks,
"Where dem chirren at?"

"Where Dem Chirren At?" was generated in collaboration with Deep Seek (AI), phrased, prompted and edited by Alvin C. Bernstine. The poem draws on thematic and stylistic elements inspired by

Langston Hughes and Paul Laurence Dunbar, but also utilizing an African American Vernacular Expression currently articulated in a popular line-dance song, "Boots on the Ground."[1] In tribute to my children, it's easy to spit with the hip hop beat. If the poetic expressions of theodicy, i.e. the Book of Job, reveals anything, it demonstrates that the poet probes more deeply into the human experience long before the thoughtful musings of the theologian. Perhaps it's because the poet is less restrained and able to say what the theologian cannot.

---

1   **"Boots on the Ground"**, also known as **"Boots on the Ground: Where Them Fans At?"** is a song written and performed by American singer Douglas Furtick, under the stage name 803Fresh, released December 2024.

Introduction

THE DRAMA:

Breaking the Silence of Mary in Black Church Life

"Silence is a strategy for the maintenance of the status quo, with its unbearable distribution of power and wealth. Silence breakers characteristically insist that the old patterns of power must be disrupted and reconfigured."

—Walter Bruggemann

[Alvin] My journey as a preacher introduced me to a world of words and concepts deemed essential for responsible Christian ministry. Theology was one of those words with its accompanying lexicon of multi-syllabic terms. Like the convoluted handshakes of secret societies and athletes' elaborate celebrations, I had to twist my tongue into palsy-like configurations to function in the academic world of theology. Initially, theological language made me feel like the demoniac in Acts 19:15: "Jesus I know, Paul I know, but who are you?" Words like *soteriology, epistemology, ecclesiology, euchology, ontology, pneumatology, eschatology,* and *Christology* challenged me because they were not the grammar used in the humble Baptist churches of my upbringing. As a late-blooming college student of the faith, I had to quickly learn the jargon or suffer the indignity of being theologically challenged, a state that my fragile ego could not easily accommodate. A consequence of pursuing words is being accused of using the "big" words I learned that remain foreign to many to whom I speak and write. To those who have been exposed to my grammatical adventures: I feel you, but words shaped my life journey and my children's. When they asked me about a word, I never gave them a single definition. I always insisted they consult the dictionaries, as I had to do myself.

One word I learned that never played in my church community was *Mariology.* Simply put, it is the study of or thoughts on Mary, the mother of Jesus. Even now, no one in my church community ever utters the word *Theotokos* or refers to Mary as "the mother of God." Such a declaration would be viewed as denominationally awkward at best, blasphemous, at worst. As a result, Mary's persona and significance are greatly diminished within my faith community. This is interesting because the utmost importance in liberation theology, particularly Black theology, is amplifying the voices of those who are historically silenced. Thankfully, Womanist theology provides a robust response to the silencing of women, often manifested in the male-dominated space of Western and Black theology. However, other than the brilliant offerings of my Nashville friend and scholar, Dr. Renita Weems, in her insightful musings in the book, *Showing Mary*[2] and Dr. Mitzi Smith, of whom we will later explore, a well-crafted theological statement that gives voice to Mary within the Black church is yet to be fully constructed. For the most part, Mary's voice remains mute within black church life and witness. This writing hopefully contributes to the amplification of Mary's voice and open discussion for a robust Black Mariology.

I confess that it took the Womanist sensitivities of my dear wife, the Honorable Reverend Diana Becton, to shift my theological lens on Mary. As she inquisitively followed the homiletical brilliance of Dr. Joel C. Gregory, she noted that for Advent 2023, he was offering Advent meditations on the Seven Sayings of Mary. I had never heard of the Seven Sayings of Mary, so this piqued my preaching curiosity. We pulled up the Seven Sayings of Mary referred to by Dr. Gregory and decided to shape our Advent 2023 preaching around Mary's words collaboratively. The plan was for Diana to preach three, I would preach three, and we would collaboratively preach one. Much to our dismay and frustration, there were scant resources on Mary from a black church perspective. There were a few offerings from the traditional Anglo-patriarchal interpretations, and we did not find white theology from black preacher-scholars compelling or relevant to Black life. In fact, we needed a Mary who identified with us. In other words, we needed to find Blackness in the drama of Mary.

After completing our preaching adventure, we both agreed to respond to Mary's glaring silence in the Black church by publishing our sermon ideas as a humble offering to the void we experienced. We also understood that sermons without some theological and historical context limit the sermon's impact. Sermons are always, in fact, theological statements. Thus, I assumed the responsibility of framing the Seven Sayings of Mary in a theological query around the historical silence of Mary, initiating the search for the powerful potential of Mariology for the liberating ministry of the Black church.

To that end, we begin by confronting what we considered a significant obstacle to Mariology in the Black church: black people's issues with sex. For sure, black people are not the only people who have issues with sex, but we leave that for others to explore. [Alvin] My hermeneutical instincts presumed that Mary having a child without a sexual experience conflicted with the racist sexualization of the Black experience. And, we both contend that the black church's timidity toward human sexuality, in general, is the consequence of severe sexual trauma experienced in enslavement, compounded by sexually confusing white theology and abusive social practices. So, the sexual issues of black people shape our opening foray of finding Blackness in the drama of Mary.

Secondly, [Alvin] I briefly muse over what Dr. Dante Quick identified as the "cultural artifacts"[3] of

2   Renita J. Weems, Showing Mary: How Women Can Share Prayers, Wisdom, and the Blessings of God (Warner Books, New York, NY, 2002)
3   Provided during teaching the class "Theology of Preaching" for the Bay Area Academy of Responsible Preaching in the Spring of 2020.

Mary in Black church life. The cultural artifacts used are viewed under the scrutiny of traditional definitions of Mariology. Thirdly, I explore the powerful insights of Womanist scholar, Dr. Mitzi Smith, and draw on her academic genius to offer suggestions for a Black Church Mariology and the potential for ministry and preaching. Fourthly, I offer a soft critique of Black Theology's "blind spot" on Mariology in contrast to Latin American Liberation's robust embrace of Mary as a primary feature of its understanding of ministry and life. Finally, since my ministry and academic life have been consumed with preaching and the methodologies thereof, the Seven Sayings of Mary, as preached, are prominently featured with accompanying questions for discussion. It is our hope that our humble sermon efforts serve as homiletical demonstrations on preaching from a Black Mariological perspective.

If we could recommend any use for this publication, we believe it would be helpful for personal enrichment, group discussions, and church Bible studies. It could also be a stimulating resource for retreats with church leaders responsible for shifting a church's culture. Or, you can do as we did, use it as a resource for preaching and help break the Mariological silence still prevalent in most of our churches.

HIDING FROM MARY AND THE VIRGIN BIRTH:
"Black People's Issues with Sex"

"Slavery provided wealthy white citizens the ability to purchase a virtually endless supply of men, women, and children to abuse in whatever manner their fancies bid them, for however long the enslaved could survive; and all with total impunity

—Joy DeGruy

We are clear that there are a myriad of possible challenges obstructing the black church's historical reluctance to a robust theological embrace of Mary, with sexism being prominent. Yet, for me, one challenge stands out—sex. Specifically, black people's experiences with sex, post-European contact, have created a formidable challenge. The traumatic disconnect between indigenous African spirituality and Eurocentric physicality created an insurmountable sexual dilemma: the bifurcation between spirit and flesh. Sobonfu Somé insightfully observed that "Once an intimate relationship is taken out of its spiritual context, it faces many dangers" (Somé, 1997, p. 17). Black sexuality taken out of its spiritual context and placed into the brutal commodification of chattel slavery and modern-day hedonism has been dangerously disruptive, to say the least. Therefore, being honest about our views and behavior patterns regarding human sexuality is critical to understanding the complexities of black people and their relationship with Mary.

A major tenet of traditional Mariology, if not the defining tenet, is the virgin birth. Even if black people have never read anything about Mary beyond Bible stories, the virgin birth, or the immaculate conception is widely known. I want to assert that virginity, as commonly perceived, is a highly charged sexual reality that complicates the eager embrace of Mariology for many black Christians. The theological elephant in the room is that the virgin birth, or the immaculate conception, is an obstructive issue because of black people's sexual experiences in America. To put it bluntly, our issues with sex and Mary as a virgin trigger those issues.

Let us be clear: our issues with sex are primarily the result of the continuing impact of dehumanization experienced through the compound trauma of centuries of enslavement, Jim Crowism, the prison industrial complex, sprinkled in with the confusion of the hippie-driven free-sex period. Adding to the trauma are the convoluted sexual views, teachings, and practices imposed upon us by White Christian colonizers and enslavers. To examine this matter, I [Alvin] offer a cursory exploration of some of the historical and psycho-social components of black people's issues with sex and its impact on Mariology in the black experience. Ann Mauro's *The Colonization of Black Sexualities: A Clinical Guide to Reclaiming and Healing* (2024) helped provide a psychosocial lens. From a clinical perspective, but with the sensitivity of a historian and public intellectual, she aptly described many of the historical and psychosocial dynamics of black sexuality. For instance, her use of the term "ethnosexuality" denotes an intersection of race/ethnicity and sexuality, and "no ethnic boundary is more sexualized, surveilled, and scrutinized in U.S. society than the color line in dividing blacks and whites" (Nagel, 2020, p. 113).

David Archer, in *Antiracist Psychotherapy: Confronting Systemic Racism and Healing Racial Trauma*, observed that, "while all forms of suffering are damaging, some appear to leave 'trauma' in the individual and scar our social orders" (Archer, 2021, p. 23). Mauro (2024) further cited Resma Menakem, who asserted, "Our very bodies house the unhealed dissonance and trauma of our ancestors" (Menakem, 2021, p. 3).

SEX BEFORE COLUMBUS

[Alvin] My worldview, including my views on sex, shifted during a recent life-changing visit to Ghana. During that visit,[4] Diana and I encountered an Africa not known through the books of our early education and never experienced in life. While I have held a lifelong curiosity about Africa and Africans before European contact, I was deeply impressed by the richness of the historical African societies. Historically, Africans possessed highly structured and communal approaches to life, politics, and sexuality. I was aware of African tribalism and spirituality but uninformed about African sexuality beyond multiple wives and "brutal" female castrations. However, during this visit, my Westernized orientation to human sexuality was radically disrupted and altered. I learned that sexuality in Africa was not an individualized responsibility but was understood within the broader framework of family, lineage, and community stability. Unlike Western individualistic notions of sexuality and marriage, African communities often approached sexual relationships as a matter of collective concern, shaped by cultural, spiritual, and economic considerations.

Sexuality in precolonial African societies was not a private affair between two people but was regulated by extended families, elders, and community institutions to maintain social harmony. All of this was firmly grounded in spirit. "There is a spiritual dimension to every relationship, no matter what its origin, whether it is acknowledged as spiritual or not. Two people come together because spirit wants them together" (Somé, 1997, p. 13). This spiritual grounding ensured that sexual relationships contributed to the well-being of the family, lineage, and society as a whole. Of particular interest in the Dagara tribe is the communal concept of spirit:

---

4 A trip taken with the Mid-Winter Judicial Council of the National Bar Association, (An African American organization of lawyers and judges.) January 18-27, 2024.

Community is the spirit, the guiding light of the tribe, whereby people come together in order to fulfill a specific purpose, to help others fulfill their purpose, and to take care of one another. …The community is that grounding place where people come together and share their gifts and receive from others. (Somé, 1997, p. 22)

My distorted, Westernized Romeo and Juliet perspective was seriously challenged by the African understanding that sexuality demanded communal oversight. Elders and extended families played a significant role in overseeing sexual relationships and marriage, ensuring that such matters aligned with cultural norms and social responsibilities. I was stunned to realize that the muted silence on sex that my parents and grandparents exposed me to was not only abnormal but an egregious departure from the norms of our African ancestry. Traditionally, elders, women for women and men for men, acted as advisors on sexuality, offering guidance on intimacy, fertility, and marital harmony. Sexual education was often transmitted through oral traditions, initiation rites, and mentorship, rather than being left to individual discovery. I shamefully confess that my primary course of learning about sex, through personal discovery or the assistance of well-meaning, but equally ignorant peers, was communally irresponsible.

According to African traditions, there was no way I should have been married when or how I was. My first wife and I unilaterally decided we wanted to get married. We decided first and sought consultation afterward, but our minds were made up. Not so in many African cultures. Marriage was a communal institution, not a legal contract made among two individuals under the guise of romantic attraction. In many African societies, marriage was not merely a personal decision but a union between families. Two young people never decided to get married on their own. Somé (1997) described marriage as "a way of taking the call of the spirit further. It brings two souls, two purposes, two worlds together, and allows them to bring their gifts forward to benefit the community" (p. 67). Elders conducted negotiations over marriage to ensure compatibility and social stability. These discussions often included economic considerations. A "bride-wealth (lobola or dowry) was common practice, symbolizing not a purchase but a means of establishing familial bonds and ensuring that the marriage benefited both lineages. Sexual relations outside of marriage were often regulated by communal expectations, though the level of strictness varied by region and ethnic group.

Much of [Alvin] my education about love and sex came through popular culture, particularly Black music. Artists like The Temptations, The O'Jays, Chi-Lites, Martha Reeves and the Vandellas, Smokey Robinson, Marvin Gaye and Tammy Terrell, Jackie Wilson, Lennie Williams, and a host of bebop and doo-doo- wop groups and entertainers. Most of the entertainers were not much older than I was, but with rhythmic seduction they harmoniously provided the lyrical curriculum for my understanding of love and sex. (I confess: I'm old school and proud of it. I never fully embraced, nor aesthetically appreciated, the overt misogynistic tones of the hip-hop crowd.) In contrast, most African societies had structured rites of passage, particularly for young men and women entering adulthood.

These rites included teachings about sexual responsibility, fertility, and the sacredness of sexuality in relation to the ancestors and the divine. For example, among the Dagara people, "the whole concept of the intimate is primarily from ritual. Outside of ritual, nothing can be truly intimate. Which is why, in the village, every emotion is ritualistically understood" (Somé, 1997, pp. 49-50). Among the Baganda of Uganda and the Zulu of South Africa, older women (often aunts or grandmothers) would educate younger women about sexual pleasure, reproductive health, and the expectations of married life.

Mauro (2024) reminded us that a basic tenet of sexological systems theory holds that, "the development of one's sexuality is the result of biological and psychological processes that are acted within a socio-cultural context, which, in turn, shapes its expressions" (Jones et. al., 2001, as cited in Mauro, 2024). Contrary to the rigid patriarchal systems imposed by European colonizers, many African societies operated on principles of gender complementarity rather than strict gender hierarchy. Sexual relations were understood within the framework of mutual benefit, where both men and women had roles in ensuring a successful union. In some cases, female sexuality was not only acknowledged but celebrated, as seen in fertility festivals and spiritual practices that honored women's reproductive power.

[Diana] When I think about sexual silence, I have to tell the truth about my own upbringing. It was stunted to say the least. My father's contribution to sex education was short and blunt: *"Keep your dress down and your panties up."* That was it. My mother—a proud but very private beautician—never said a word. My grandmother, if the subject even came close, would just giggle like a schoolgirl.

When I asked my four best girlfriends—the women I've known since grade school, over sixty years—what they were told, their stories echoed mine. Two received the *exact same words* from their fathers. One, raised by a single mother, received nothing at all. And another was told, *"Stay away from boys and keep your legs closed."* She told me she was twelve years old, walking through East Oakland, trying to figure out how in the world a girl could walk with her legs closed.

Meanwhile, when women came to my mother's salon, they poured out their hearts—troubles with men, worries about their children, heartbreaks they carried like extra weight in their purses. We weren't supposed to listen, but my sisters and I would sneak to the cracked door, straining to catch every whispered confession.

And then, miraculously, one day while our parents were out, my sisters and I "found" a hidden book about anatomy—men's and women's bodies laid out in diagrams. We pulled it out like treasure, giggling and gasping, sneaking an education our parents never gave us.

That was my introduction to sex: a father's warning, a mother's silence, a grandmother's giggle, the overheard laments of women under the hot comb, the whispered advice of girlfriends, and the secret pages of a book.

So when I sat in seminary years later, and professors spoke of *Mariology*—the virgin birth, *Theot-*

okos, immaculate conception—I felt the gap inside me. What did these "big words" mean for girls like me? For women raised in silence, who learned through whispers and shadows?

If we are to talk about Mary, we cannot tiptoe around sexual silence and its traumatic sources. We must name it, break it, and listen for her voice in the very places where women have always been speaking—sometimes behind cracked doors.

We have recently put a lot of the music and lyrics of our youth under the serious scrutiny of my advanced age, education, and lived experiences. Admittedly, we have found ways to still enjoy the music and the intent behind many of those songs. For instance, [Alvin] I love the rhythm and beat of *Poppa Was a Rolling Stone* but cannot embrace the lyrics because my father's experience does not connect with it. My father was a cornerstone, not a rolling stone. He was present, and when he was no longer physically present, I knew where to locate him, both physically and morally. Likewise, we have a hard time celebrating the objectification, sexual suppression, and impotence of women in many popular songs. This becomes highly problematic when juxtaposed with the prominence of black women in our communities and the sexual agency found in our African ancestry.

The image portrayed by women in Africa, prior to European contact, was not one of submissive objectification, sexual suppression, or a lack of personal sexual agency. On the contrary, African women in many precolonial societies exercised significant sexual agency. This agency manifested in various ways, including autonomy in partner selection, female-led sexual traditions, and the ability to negotiate sexual relationships. While arranged marriages were common, many African societies allowed women a say in choosing their partners. Women in some ethnic groups, such as the Wolof of Senegal and the Akan of Ghana, held the right to refuse suitors. In matrilineal societies such as the Ashanti and the Bemba, women had greater control over marriage and divorce, reinforcing their sexual autonomy.

[Alvin] I grew up with six sisters (one now deceased), and from my observations, none of them appeared to function with a sexual awareness noticeably different from mine. My mother struggled with her own sexual issues, so I doubt she handed down sexual wisdom to her daughters. And, as stated above Diana and her two sisters stumbled upon a human anatomy book that pierced the glaring silence of their parents. However, the women in Africa were taught from a young age about their bodies, pleasure, and reproductive choices, often through female elders or secret societies. Among the Bantu-speaking groups, for instance, women participated in initiation schools where they learned about sexual expression and the power dynamics of relationships. "During initiation, you learn about many things; sex and intimacy are just a part of the teachings. Even after the initiation, there is a long period of mentoring" (Somé, 1997, p. 42).

While less common than polygyny, some African societies also permitted polyandry or accepted structures where women had multiple sexual partners. In societies like the Lovedu of South Africa, women in positions of power (such as queens or female chiefs) could take multiple husbands or lovers without social stigma. Female husbands (as seen among the Igbo and Kikuyu) were another example of women's sexual agency. A woman could marry another woman for lineage purposes, sometimes engaging in sexual relations with male partners of her choosing to produce heirs. This arrangement carried no moral shame nor was she labeled a whore.

Other expressions of sexual agency among women were evident in divorce, birth control, and religion. Divorce was widely accepted in many African cultures if a marriage was unfulfilling or the husband failed in his duties. Among the Yoruba and Hausa, women could return to their families or seek new partners if a marriage was not working. Women also had control over their reproductive lives, often engaging in herbal contraceptive practices or making decisions about childbirth. In some African spiritual systems, women served as priestesses, mediums, and healers, often involving elements of sacred sexuality. Some rituals involved sexual expression as a means of divine communication or fertility invocation, showing that female sexuality was not viewed as sinful but as a powerful, life-giving force. Rituals, intimacy, and sexuality were inextricable dynamics of what it meant to be a woman or a man.

So, what does all of that have to do with Mary? It matters much because most of us have imposed the distorted, Westernized, individualized, Romeo and Juliet romantic perspective upon the biblical text. We have hermeneutically assumed that the individualized sexual practices of America culturally describe the Joseph and Mary relationship. Some of us probably believe they dated and listened to the latest Jewish love songs under a romantic moon. However, ancient Jewish marriage practices, including engagement, were more closely aligned with the African tradition. Like Africans, marriages were highly communal and involved specific family expectations.

In Jesus's day, marriage was far more than a private contract between two individuals; it was an event that involved families, extended kin, and the broader community. Consider the wedding at Cana in John 2. The bride is never mentioned by name, yet the entire community is present. The wine crisis was resolved by community members, with the father of the bride asking the unnamed bridegroom about the wine's quality (John 2:9). Like in many African cultures, marriage served as an alliance between families, reinforcing social ties and economic stability. Decisions were typically made not solely by the couple but by their families, who considered factors like lineage, social standing, and religious observance.

The world in which Mary lived betrothal (or *kiddushin*) was a formal, legally binding phase that preceded the marriage ceremony. This process was characterized by its communal and contractual nature. Parents or guardians negotiated matches that aligned with the community's values, ensuring that the union would not only sustain but also enhance the collective honor and continuity of the people. While not absent, love was often considered secondary to considerations of duty, heritage, and mutual family benefit. Communal honor and shame trumped amorous affections and intents.

Moreover, marriage in ancient Judaism was deeply embedded in the community's religious identity. It was seen as a means of fulfilling divine commandments and preserving the covenantal identity of the Jewish people. The union of husband and wife was understood to contribute to the communal project of maintaining religious traditions and societal order. As such, marriages were celebrated and regulated by both civil and religious authorities, ensuring that individual unions reinforced communal values. I once officiated a wedding between a Black woman and a Jewish young man. It was a collaborative ceremony, Christians and Jews, with a Jewish Rabbi as co-officiant. The couple even smashed the wine glass, as required in Jewish tradition.

Perhaps the visitations of the angels to Mary in *Luke* and Joseph in *Matthew* implied "Spirit" involvement and communal connections as attested in the genealogies. However, our ethnocentric blind spots and cultural incompetence prevent us from considering the communal significance of the ancient Jewish family dynamics. Mary and Joseph would have never unilaterally dealt with a pre-marital crisis as severe as a scandalous pre-marital pregnancy in isolation, even one cloaked in God-talk. We could consider the visit to Elizabeth as the storyteller's implication of communal involvement. Nevertheless, interestingly, Joseph was never mentioned during the visit with Elizabeth. Moreover, the Elizabeth visit never explicitly addressed the obvious and/or assumed crisis of Mary's pre-marital pregnancy. Elizabeth, as a representative of the community, celebrated with and provided comfort to Mary in her prophetically inspired pregnancy.

In stark contrast, modern Western views of marriage place a premium on individual choice, romantic love, and sexual intimacy. Marriage is often viewed as a private, emotionally driven contract between two individuals, regulated by legal and moral frameworks emphasizing personal fulfillment and autonomy. This interpretation reconfigures the Nativity narrative of marital relations into one centered on individual desire and emotional connection.

E. Randolph Richards and Brandon J. O'Brien, in their insightful book *Misreading Scripture Western Eyes*, warned us of the distortions created when we indiscriminately interpret the biblical text (Richards & O'Brien, 2012). The biases of "Western eyes" as the cultural lens through which Western readers interpret the Bible are too often shaped by unacknowledged assumptions and values such as individualism, moralism, absolutism, and self-centeredness. These biases often distort biblical interpretation by imposing modern Western perspectives onto ancient texts, which were written in communal, honor-shame, and relational contexts. No bias is more evident than Westerners' tendency to prioritize rules over relationships and interpret Scripture through an individualistic framework rather than understanding its collective implications.

We believe that the cultural context of Joseph and Mary's marriage, while compromised by Roman oppression, was rooted in communal obligations and religious purpose. Over time, however, Western interpretations projected an idealized, individual-driven, romantic partnership onto their relationship. This culturally imposed shift obscured the original understanding that their union was primarily about fulfilling a communal role—protecting lineage, upholding covenantal identity, and serving a broader social purpose.

In addition, colonialism distorted indigenous sexual systems and marital practices by super-imposing Western, patriarchal, and moralistic standards that undermined communal regulation of sexuality and restricted women's sexual freedom. These distortions also shaped a Mariology infused with patriarchal, racist, and sexist assumptions. Imani Perry (2018), in *Vexy Thing: On Gender and Liberation*, believed that patriarchy's formation took three judicial forms: sovereignty, property, and personhood. Patriarchy advanced the notion of the yielders of power (sovereignty) based upon the holders of property, which included slaves, women, and children, who determined who was a person or a nonperson.

Murro (2020) explained, "The need to have order in social relationships unfortunately helped foster a hierarchy to measure a person's status as 'person, man, woman, freeman, negro, slave.' Sadly, personhood and citizenship were tied directly to property, since you could not own land if you were not a 'person' or a 'citizen.' In order to protect their property, men were motivated to join political society to ensure protection of land and property" (p. 14).

THE ELEPHANT IN THE ROOM – The Virgin Mary Dilemma

Perry's (2018) observation on patriarchy provides a template for deepening our understanding of virginity and what it symbolizes. Departing from our usual way of constructing an essay, sermon, legal brief, or argument, we begin with a conclusion. The issue of virginity, particularly as imposed upon Mary, the mother of Jesus, represents a cultural construct of patriarchy to add value to property, specifically white women and indirectly diminish the value enslaved Black women. Virginity, in this framework, supports patriarchy's intention to maintain judicial control of sovereignty, property, and personhood. Simply put: who else would use a woman's body to determine her worth and value in a patriarchal society? White men, promoting patriarchy and white supremacy, imposed value on women's bodies, created and perpetuated the virginity complex.

Virginity, as a construct of patriarchy, converts the prerogatives of a woman's body into the sexual preferences of men. Murro (2020) referenced a recent Netflix series, Bridgerton, where significant drama revolved around the chastity of women. She stated, "Language worked to reinforce this assumption that a 'pure virgin' was much more valuable than a 'dirty whore'" (Murro, 2020, p. 17). This issue becomes more complicated and insidious when connected to racism and the commodification of Black bodies.

Having begun where we hoped to end, we present the cultural premises. In the days of Jesus, the ancient Near Eastern world, including first-century Jewish culture, virginity was primarily understood in terms of sexual purity and social honor. A virgin (Hebrew: *betulah*; Greek: *parthenos*) was an unmarried woman who had not had sexual relations. Virginity was closely tied to family honor, economic stability, and social status. A woman's virginity was seen as a valuable asset, ensuring her eligibility for marriage and safeguarding her family's reputation. Marriage was often arranged, and virginity was a prerequisite for betrothal and marriage. A woman's lack of virginity before marriage led to severe consequences, including public shaming or even death (Deuteronomy 22:13-21).

In the Hebrew Bible, virginity was often used symbolically to represent purity, faithfulness, and devotion to God, when in reality it was a cultural consideration used to uphold patriarchy. Women, although objectified, interestingly bore the burden of having their bodies used as symbols of faithfulness. In patriarchal societies, a family's honor was closely tied to the behavior of its female members. A woman's virginity was seen as a reflection of her family's moral integrity and social standing. For example, Israel is described as a virgin bride in her covenantal relationship with Yahweh (e.g., Ezekiel 16:8-14; Jeremiah 2:2). Virginity was not merely a private matter but a public concern. Proof of virginity (e.g., the presence of a hymen) was sometimes required in cases of dispute (Deuteronomy 22:13-21). Understandably, widows and divorced women were not brought under the scrutiny of virginity, even if they had not remarried, as virginity was tied to the state of being unmarried and sexually inexperienced.

According to traditional interpretations, Mary's virginity (Matthew 1:18-25; Luke 1:26-38) is emphasized in the New Testament as a sign of divine intervention and the fulfillment of prophecy (Isaiah 7:14). Her virginity, when presented as a moral concern and not a communal expectation, underscores the miraculous nature of Jesus' birth and his unique identity as the Son of God. Of note, however, is that in traditional Western societies, particularly in medieval and early modern Europe, virginity was also highly valued but took on additional moral and religious connotations influenced by Westernized patriarchal Christianity. It became associated with celibacy and asceticism, particularly in the context of monasticism and the veneration of saints. In addition, virginity was seen as a higher spiritual state, reflecting purity and dedication to God. The Virgin Mary became a central figure in Western Christianity, and her perpetual virginity (the belief that she remained a virgin before, during, and after the birth of Jesus) was emphasized as a model of holiness. This belief took on a theological life of its own, with no regard for the Jewish cultural context and history. It also served as a moral standard imaged in white femaleness and an obstacle to the humanization of black women.

ENSLAVEMENT AND BEYOND

In this strange age of anti-wokeness and revisionist history, Black people must assume the responsibility of telling our own story. Like the Jews and the Holocaust, just because some people believe our enslavement is best forgotten, we should never forget. We cannot forget because our bodies and our troubled relationship with sex remember. Edward Baptist (2014) aptly observed, "Slavery's frontier was a white man's sexual playground" (p. 238).

Our bodies will forever testify to the horrific commodification of enslavement and its consequent impact upon our psyche and sexuality. Dr. Bessel Van Der Kolk helps us in his amazing study on how the body keeps trauma in the present long after it has past.[5] I was personally re-traumatized upon entering the slave cells in Ghana, and was told the horrors of sexual exploitation that began prior to the Middle Passage. Many of these slave cells were built within close proximity to white churches, and the leaders of the church shared in inflicting sexual trauma upon helpless enslaved Black people. While the popular stories imply White males objectifying Black females, we must include sexual assaults upon Black males from degenerate White males.

Enslaved Black women, as well as Black men, were subjected to sexual violence and exploitation by White slaveholders. The point being that white supremacy reached its evil tentacles into every aspect of Black life, including human sexuality. The myth of the "Jezebel" stereotype, where Black women were portrayed as being hypersexual, was used to justify their abuse. Any deviant sexual appetite possessed by White men was rationalized by the lie that Black women were not fully human and therefore incapable of experiencing any moral outrage, even when evident in their faces and by their physical resistance.

Likewise, the emasculation of Back men served to further the embedded fears of white supremacy, and the fear of Black men's sexual prowess exposed the sexual fragility of White men. Black men were stripped of autonomy and often portrayed as hypermasculine or sexually threatening, thus, advancing the "Black Brute," or "Mandingo" stereotype.

Murro (2020) explained, "Slavery violated the masculinity of Black men who were denied the ability to protect vulnerable female dependents" (p. 19). She added that "bystander trauma occurs when an individual watches someone go through a traumatic event" (p. 19), such as the rape or forced sexual advances of white men upon Black women. Although laws formally prohibited sexual contact between races, Solomon (2017) argued that these laws functioned less as protection for white women and more as reinforcement of white dominance. In practice, many white women, particularly those who were slaveholders or the wives of enslavers, also exploited Black men, often in retaliation for their husbands' infidelities with Black women. Murro (2020) pointed out, "The truth is that enslaved Black men were sexually assaulted by white people, and this has been mostly ignored" (p. 22). In today's climate of historical denial, such truths continue to be suppressed.

Thomas Foster (2018) detailed the specific forms of abuse suffered by Black men during slavery, including "penetrative assault, forced reproduction, sexual coercion and manipulation, and psychic abuse" (p. 125). Such explains the sick and sadistic behavior of New York police, who in 1997, assaulted Abner Louima by viciously plunging a broken broomstick in his rectum and then into his mouth. This was more egregious than police brutality. It was the continued assault upon Black male masculinity and sexuality.

---

5   Bessel Van Der Kolk M.D., The Body Keeps the Score: Brain, Mind, and Body in the Healing of Trauma, (Penguin Books, New York, New York, 2014.

The rabid fear of black male sexuality was used to justify lynching and other forms of racial violence. While visiting an African American Museum in Maryland, [Alvin] I recall viewing the bottled display of "Black genitals" immersed in embalming fluids, eerily preserved as tokens of white fear during the hateful rituals of lynchings. Somewhere in the twisted psyche of white supremacy, the brutal castrations of Black men propped up their fragile egos.

Jokes and tragedies abound around the white fear of Black men's sexual prowess. The great African American comic, Richard Pryor, once joked in searing satire that the reason Black men were often seen clutching their crotches was because "you [white men] took everything else, [motherf$cker]!" In 1927, John Carter was brutally lynched, shot over 200 times, and his castrated body burned from the chopped-up pews of the Bethel African Methodist Episcopal Church in Little Rock, Arkansas. All of this occurred after he was dragged by the neck down Main Street before cheering white onlookers. Such extreme brutality, compounded with the desecration of the sacred, served notice to any and every resistant Black that nothing Black, bodies or churches, were excluded from the domain of white supremacy. This message was further demonstrated when fourteen-year-old Emmett Till was brutally beaten, castrated, and shot by white Mississippians over the unjustified white fear of Black male sexuality. The tragic drama of both was played out by white women's fragile sense of self, being sexually exploited to gain a diminished sense of sexual agency.

We hold that the greatest contributor to the sexual issues of black people has been white people's Christianity. Jesus warned the people of his oppressed community, "Do not fear those who kill the body but cannot kill the soul. Rather, fear him who can destroy both soul and body in hell" (Matthew 10:28, ESV). Such a warning to black people would caution us to have more fear of a white man with a Bible than a white man with a gun. Black people's embrace of a version of Christianity intended to control, oppress, and sexually emasculate further blurs and complicates our views on human sexuality, inevitably skewing a wholesome and welcoming understanding of Mary. Accepting white Christianity's commitment to patriarchy's template of sovereignty, property, and personhood (as noted earlier) gets in the way because it reinforce[s] "the man in a higher position of power placing the father in the position of father to care and rule over his family, thus mimicking the ruling powers and God, operating as a commonwealth of ruling powers that protected his kin and property" (Murro, 2020, p. 14).

Unless we choose to remain oblivious to black church history, we must accept the historical fact that white Christians imposed a brand of Christianity as a psychological tool for social control. "Christianity was imposed on the enslaved Africans to bring them under psychological submission to white domination. It was never for their salvation, at least among planters, for it was widely conceded that Africans did not have a soul (Williams, 2022, p. 27)."

In the history of the Pleasant Hill Baptist Church, Heflin, Louisiana, a church organized on the Heflin Plantation by my [Alvin] enslaved matriarchal ancestors, it was noted that "the white preacher would come on some Sundays and sit in the back of the church to listen. While he acted like he was enjoying the service, we knew he was there to keep his eyes on us."[6] Why was he keeping eyes on black worshippers? It was clear to the Black worshippers that he wanted to make sure they remained faithful to the oppressive preachments of white Christianity imposed upon them. They understood that any deviation from the theological scripts of white Christianity was a social threat and would be immediately and violently discouraged.

Before I [Alvin] ever heard of Black theology, I held the primary tenets of White Christianity espoused by the Black church in suspicion. Those tenets so passionately embraced by black preachers, particularly those in my community, always seemed inadequate for the challenges of black life. The primary tenets of white Christianity were, and remain: individualized salvation, or being "born again," moral living, which most often meant obeying white laws, sexual "purity," and heavenly rewards. Sexual "purity" was confusing, given the widespread liberty white men took with black women.

An emphasis on moral living as a religious tenet ignores the teachings of Jesus, who defied those who claimed moral superiority (John 8:2-12). Jesus admonished us to aspire to do what is right and just, but not at the expense of judging others. Our moral obligation should always be for the greater good of the black community and not for the benefit of white laws designed to oppress. The concept of "being born again" needs serious theological reimagining for it to mean more than repeating a white-framed litany without a commitment to the liberation of black people.

[Alvin] I suspect that no tenet of Western Christianity has done more to distort what it means to be a follower of Jesus than that of individualized salvation. Reducing the liberating witness of Jesus to a once-stated encounter (John 3:3) is not only absurd but grossly misleading. The word used for "born again" in the John text literally means to be born from above, which might suggest being born above the oppressive constructs of a colonized power. Yet, making a single statement the central objective of what it means to be a disciple ignores everything else Jesus taught, especially about loving one's neighbor with the same regard one has for oneself.

White supremacy's vision of rugged individualism further corrupted Christianity to justify unchecked greed, selfishness, and the quest for power, including sexual power. When white supremacy reduces communal concerns to that which only aligns with the concerns of the individual, it inevitably diminishes the humanity of those who might be different by race, gender, culture, or class. Yet, the issue of sexual purity for black people cannot be discussed without acknowledging the sexual trauma inflicted upon us by those who promoted the concept. My parents were from Louisiana, which was a notorious slave-breeding state. Like prized horses and cattle, black people were forced to mate with no regard for intimacy or family.

Murro (2020) stated, "Many men were forced into marriages where their partners did not consent to be with them. They were forced to have sex, at times at gunpoint, to impregnate their unwilling wife.

---

6   In 1996, I read this in a copy of a church record's book while visiting my uncle James Miles, a deacon of Pleasant Hill Baptist Church.

For such men, the rejection and resentment of their forced wives would have further compounded their dehumanizing situation" (p. 45). Breeding slaves accomplished the same goals as breeding cattle and horses: the more enslaved children born, the greater the wealth of the enslaver. The social consequences of forced breeding trauma continue to impact Black family life.

[Alvin] I recently attended a funeral where one man had fathered eleven children with several different women. Is it any wonder black men can have children from multiple women and never be a "father" to any of them? The same could be said of black women. Having a baby does not make you a mother when your raison d'être was to breed instead of parent. Using black women for breeding covered a multitude of white sins and further justified their dehumanization.

Nzegwu (2011) explained that "Black women were portrayed as more sexual, less moral, less beautiful, less delicate and such claims allegedly excused rape, the rejection of children, the sale of lovers, and the practice of forcing black women to labor in jobs for which white women were too delicate" (p. 255). Sexual purity was a concept not meant for black people, but for the racist idolatry of "reconstituting white women into paragons of purity and beauty and deserving love and affection, and fetishized non-white bodies as expendable and worthless" (Nzegwu, 2011, p. 255). Within this racist paradigm of Western Christianity, Mary, the Mother of Jesus, was situated in the whiteness of white women, thereby making it difficult for the Black church to embrace and/or relate to her as do our Latin brothers and sisters. We will discuss the role of Mary in the lives of our Latin brothers and sisters in the section on Theology, where we also consider Dr. Mitzi Smith's "doule" perspective as a challenge to traditional Mariology and an opportunity for a Black Mariology. We now segue to Dr. Smith and her provocative perspective on Mary as a "doule", and consider the implications thereof for a power Black Mariology.

IS YOU GOT GOOD RELIGION?
We've argued that the tepid embrace of Mariology, the theological study and accompanying silence of Mary, among black Christians should be understood through the historical, cultural, and religious dynamics outlined in the previous sections. The intersection of race, sexuality, and Western Christianity shaped Black Christian theology and practice in ways that often distance it from certain aspects of Catholic and other so-called "High-Church" traditions, particularly Mariology. It seems Dolores Williams (1993) placed her theological finger on the matter when she cited Asian feminist, Chun Hyun Kyung who described the androcentric rendition of Mary to be "alien … because she is either too clean, too high, and too holy or she is too sweet, too passive and too forgiving" (p. 179). In contrast, Williams added that "Black women were construed by social mythology to be loose, immoral, incapable of either innocence or purity" (p. 180).

Without question, the intersection of sexuality and moral respectability with Mariology props up the idolatry of patriarchy. Mariology and the idealization of virginity reinforce patriarchal and repressive views of women's sexuality. As depicted in Western theology, the Virgin Mary is often portrayed as the epitome of sexual purity and motherhood, which creates a tension with the lived experiences of black people, particularly with Black women whose lived experiences consisted of one expression of sexual objectification after another. For instance, the hypersexualization of black women (e.g., the "Jezebel" stereotype) contrasts sharply with the idealized purity of Mary, creating a disconnect between Mariology and the lived experiences of Black women.

The theological pressure to conform to Eurocentric norms while ignoring and minimizing our African heritage is inevitably dissonant. Black churches have often embraced respectability politics, promoting behaviors and values that align with white, middle-class norms, including conservative views on sexuality. I [Alvin] recall a prominent preacher in our church community who never preached a sermon without alluding to the convoluted sexual prohibitions advanced by white people. In my nearly fifty years of preaching, I have yet to encounter that much sex in the Bible, or at least not enough to warrant its mention in every sermon! I observed and discovered that every young preacher under his tutelage later struggled with some form of sexual confusion. This obsession with sex from the pulpit magnifies our contention that Black people have issues with sex, and those issues significantly shape our view of Mary.

Perhaps, the Marian devotion, with its emphasis on Mary's perpetual virginity, may be seen as reinforcing Eurocentric ideals of femininity that exclude or marginalize Black women.

Dr. Mitzi Smith provides a perspective pregnant with Black Mariological possibilities when she alludes to Mary as a *"doule,"* an enslaved woman.[7] Her provocative depiction of Mary as an enslaved woman aligns Mary more closely to the lived experiences of black women than the idolatrous idealization of white women. She also situates Mary in a social space that not only mocks the idolatry of the pure white woman but also does the Womanist thing of unmasking, debunking, and disentangling.[8] By framing Mary as an enslaved woman, Smith draws a powerful connection between Mary's historical and social context and the experiences of enslaved African American women. This powerful reimagining is antithetical to the passive, idealized Mary of white patriarchal theology, which often portrays her as a symbol of purity, submission, and white womanhood.

With embarrassing brevity, I [Alvin] offer a summary of Dr. Smith's powerful portrayal of Mary as a *doule* and consider how it aligns with the experiences of enslaved African American women and critiques the traditional, idealized Mary. I will conclude by offering a few of its implications for a Black Mariology. Dr. Smith established her hermeneutical lens by noting that "to be contextually relevant, all Scriptures require interpretation or translation to function as good news for a particular person or community" (Smith, 2022, p. 54). I have long believed that for Black people to get something different

---

7   Mitzi J. Smith, Angela N. Parker, and Erika S. Dunbar Hill, Bitter the Chastening Rod: African Biblical Interpretation After Stony the Road We Tod in the Age of BLM, SAYHERNAME, AND METOO, (Lexington Books/Fortress Academic, Lanham, Maryland, 2022), pp. 53-70.

8   A concept shares by Dr. Donna Allen in her teaching on Womanist Preaching, Spring 2020.

from the Bible, we must start seeing something different in the text, other than the racially toxic interpretations of white people. Smith strengthened my position when she further insisted that:

> Within the ideological and pseudo-anthropological economy of blackness, Africana peoples must sift through the broken shards of whitened Scriptures and biblical interpretations pressed and impressed upon us as God's word to re-imagine and repurpose the useful and resurrect a God who created all human beings equal and free. (Smith, 2022, p. 55)

Smith's reframes Mary as a *doule*, a term that explicitly denotes enslavement rather than the more sanitized or domesticated notion of a "female servant" or "helper" espoused by traditional Western interpretation. This reframing more accurately situates Mary within the oppressive socio-political structures of her time, emphasizing her marginalized status as a poor, colonized Jewish woman under Roman rule. Rome's colonization of Israel reduced the Jews to slaves of the empire, vassals to the Emperor.

By identifying Mary as an enslaved person, Smith centered her vulnerability and suffering within the institution of slavery that has always dehumanized and perpetrated violence for the "purpose of nation-building, productivity, and profits" (Smith, 2022). This portrayal challenges the traditional image of Mary as a passive, ethereal figure and instead positions her as an active participant in the struggle for liberation. In the gospel of Luke, Mary self-identifies herself as a virgin (1:34) and as an enslaved female (1:38). We first read of it when the Angel Gabriel confronts her. Smith observed that Mary brings attention to it again in the *Magnificat* (1:48).

I am intrigued by the depth of Dr. Smith's scholarly findings on slavery under Roman rule. It is certainly not scholarship that she created or invented, but scholarship ignored or blinded by white patriarchy. Smith further suggested that it is possible that Mary was owned by Joseph because there is no record of Mary and Joseph being married. She furthered her argument by stating, "I propose that Joseph could have been a freedman or freeborn master. Either way, Joseph would have owned and been engaged to the young, virginal *doule*. Both enslaved and freed persons sometimes owned slaves in antiquity" (Smith, 2022, p. 60).

One of the most amazing observations of Dr. Smith's essay is her use of the *Magnificat* (Luke 1:46-55) and Paul's presentation of the *Christ Hymn* **in Philippians 2:5-11**. Both texts, in her interpretation, reflect the experiences of marginalized and enslaved people, emphasizing God's preferential option for the poor and oppressed. In the *Magnificat*, Mary proclaims God's revolutionary action in lifting up the lowly, filling the hungry, and bringing down the powerful (Luke 1:52-53). Both songs highlight the *doule* as agents of God's great reversal. Smith challenged the traditional interpretation to metaphorically spiritualize the concept of slavery as servant.

She strengthens her assertions by stating, "The addition of the words 'of God' does not automatically preclude the material reality of enslavement" (p. 61). Smith viewed it as a radical declaration of

God's solidarity with the oppressed, aligning Mary's song with the struggles of enslaved and marginalized communities. Likewise, the *Christ Hymn* in Philippians 2 provides a reflection on Jesus' enslavement and exaltation. Just as Jesus took on the form of a slave (δοῦλος, *doulos*) and was exalted by God, Mary's *Magnificat* celebrates God's exaltation of the lowly and enslaved. Both texts emphasize God's power to transform systems of domination and to uplift those who are oppressed.

Unlike the traditional images of Mary used to idolize white women, Smith's portrayal of Mary as a *doule* resonates deeply with the experiences of enslaved African American women, who endured systemic violence, exploitation, and dehumanization. Like Mary, black women were forced into roles of servitude and labor, yet they demonstrated remarkable resilience, agency, and resistance. Enslaved African American women were frequently subjected to the dual oppression of racism and sexism, much like Mary's experience as a marginalized woman in a patriarchal, imperial context. Smith's reimagining of Mary as a *doule* thus creates a powerful theological bridge between Mary's story and the lived realities of enslaved Black women, centering their struggles and triumphs in the narrative of faith.

Traditional Mariology, shaped by white patriarchal theology, often portrays Mary as a passive, obedient, and idealized figure. She is depicted as a virgin who submits unquestioningly to God's will, embodying purity, humility, and docility. Unfortunately, this image has been weaponized to reinforce patriarchal norms and to idealize white womanhood as the standard of virtue. In contrast, Smith's Mary as a *doule* is anything but passive. Her enslavement situates her within a context of struggle and resistance, thus challenging the romanticized and depoliticized image of Mary. This portrayal rejects the notion of Mary as a symbol of submissive femininity and instead presents her as a figure of strength, agency, and defiance.

Perhaps Mary's "yes" to God (Luke 1:38) is not a passive acceptance of her fate but an active, courageous decision to participate in God's liberatory mission. This aligns with how enslaved Black women resisted their oppression through acts of survival, care, and rebellion. Smith's Mary becomes a co-laborer with God in the work of liberation, challenging the traditional portrayal of Mary as a mere vessel for divine action. This reimagining highlights the active role of marginalized women in the divine plan, affirming their dignity and power.

Smith's reimagining of Mary as a *doule* has profound theological implications for liberation theology. For one, it affirms the sacredness of marginalized women's experiences and challenges the church to confront its complicity in systems of oppression. By aligning Mary with enslaved black women, Smith calls us to consider a theology rooted in the realities of suffering and resistance as embodied in black women. This challenges traditional Mariology to move beyond abstract ideals and engage with the concrete struggles of oppressed communities.

As a path toward developing a Black Mariology, I suggest a theological immersion into the Mariology espoused by the oppressed brothers and sisters of the Latinx communities. Their vigorous embrace of Mary as being identified with the struggles of those being stomped on by the empire theologically connects with the Black experience. Dr. Smith's identification of Mary as *doule* incarnates her into what she referred to as the Blackened experience. Also, Mary, as a Blackened woman, turns traditional Mariology on its theological head and dismantles the idolatrous presentation of white women. Perhaps white women could be invited into the Blackened Mary experience and locate their own suffering and pain as being just as palpable as Black women's.

In summary, Smith's portrayal of Mary as a *doule* radically reinterprets traditional Mariology and challenges the passive, idealized image of Mary perpetuated by white patriarchal theology. By aligning Mary with the experiences of enslaved Blackened women, Smith centers the struggles and resilience of marginalized communities and critiques the ways traditional Mariology has been used to uphold systems of oppression. This reimagining transforms our understanding of Mary and calls for a theology of liberation deeply rooted in the realities of suffering, resistance, and hope common to Blackened women.

DISCUSSION QUESTIONS

1. What are your thoughts about the historical issues that Black people have with sex based upon the sexual trauma of enslavement?

2. Do you agree with the author's position on how the traditional depiction of Mary as being sexually pure serves to idealize white women?

3. How has your church community presented Mary as a perpetual virgin?

4. What would be different in your community if marital relationships rediscovered the communal connection for our African heritage?

5. How does Mitzi Smith's depiction of Mary as a slave impact your interpretation of Mary?

Chapter 2

OH MARY, DON'T YOU WEEP

Theology Matters
"Politics can be the graveyard of the poet. And only poetry can be his/her resurrection."
—Langston Hughes

CULTURAL ARTIFACTS – The Stuff Black People Create

As we understand it, cultural artifacts are tangible and intangible objects, practices, or expressions that embody a community's values, traditions, and lived experiences. Cultural artifacts serve as carriers of history, identity, and cultural memory. In the African American community, cultural artifacts are expressed through storytelling, music genres such as spirituals, blues, jazz, and hip-hop; oral traditions; culinary practices; fashion; and art forms like quilting and sculpture. They could also include significant texts, speeches, and religious practices rooted in African spirituality and Christian traditions, as well as social movements and activism that reflect resilience and the struggle for liberation. Included in cultural artifacts are the literary creations used to give emotional expression to the various aspects of Black life. The most common forms of these artifacts are expressed through song, litany, and literary prose. For the purpose of this section, we consider how Mary is made present, silenced, or heard within the cultural artifacts of Blackness.

As [Alvin] I searched for the lyrics of the song, *O Mary Don't You Weep*, it became clear that there are several renditions, each shaped by the artists' preferences. The reason for the variety of renditions is that the song was composed during the African American enslavement period, a time when most of our songs were composed and passed along through the oral tradition. There was no standard version written down for all to follow. As such, the creative distinctions of the once enslaved were shaped by the orality of their respective regions. My enslaved family ancestors suffered under the harsh cruelties of Louisiana slaveholders, so the rendition that I was introduced to was presented by the migrant quartet singers who performed in local churches. It was a rendition made popular through the melodious harmonies of the Swan Silvertones, who ironically came from the brutal coal mines of West Virginia. That rendition is as follows:

> Oh, I'm singing ... Mary (Oh Mary, don't you weep),
> Martha don't have to moan (Oh Martha, don't you moan),
> Listen to me ... Mary (Oh Mary, don't you weep),
> Martha don't have to moan (Oh Martha, don't you moan),

Pharaoh's army (Oh Mary, don't you weep),

They got drowned in the sea one day (Down in the Red Sea)

But Jesus said, "Mary." (Oh Mary, don't you weep),

You're little ole sister don't have to moan no more,

(Oh, Martha, don't you moan.)

African American folklorist John Work, whose father sang with the Fisk Jubilee Singers, included the traditional words and music in his classic American Negro Songs (Work, 1940).

O Mary, don't you weep, don't you mourn.

O Mary, don't you weep, don't you mourn.

Pharaoh's army got drowned, O Mary, don't you weep.

Aretha Franklin wrapped the song in the soulful vernacular of her "Queen of Soul" gifts by adding:

Oh, Mary, don't you weep, don't you mourn

Oh, Mary, don't you weep, don't you mourn

Didn't Pharaoh's army get drowned?

Oh, Mary, don't you weep

Well, Satan got mad, and he knows I'm glad

Missed that soul that he thought he had

Now, didn't Pharaoh's army get drowned?

Oh, Mary, don't you weep

Oh, Mary, don't you weep, don't you mourn

Oh, Mary, don't you weep, don't you mourn

Didn't Pharaoh's army get drowned?

Oh, Mary, don't you weep

However presented, this song is not about Mary, the mother of Jesus. It references Mary of Bethany (John 11) following the death of her brother Lazarus. Enslaved Africans used this story to admonish the enslaved archetypes of grief-stricken Mary and her sister Martha not to allow grief to destroy them. As ominous as was the grief of the enslaved, they were encouraged to anticipate deliverance from the clutches of death by enslavement, just as their freedom-seeking spiritual ancestors did at the Red Sea. As an enslaved people, they used the encouragement of Mary of Bethany to encourage themselves, as they hopefully anticipated the destruction of the death-dealing forces that held them captive.

I mention this song because of its prevalence in Black church life, where it is not uncommon for people to confuse Mary of Bethany with Mary, Jesus's mother. It is safe to assume they knew each other, but the message of the enslaved Africans was to connect any and every grief-stricken oppressed person with the hope of deliverance from any and every death-dealing construct.

Another cultural artifact that absolutely includes Mary, the mother of Jesus, is *Go Tell It on the*

Mountain. African American spirituals and carols celebrating the Nativity often center on Mary's humble obedience and divine calling.

> Go, tell it on the mountain
> Over the hills and everywhere
> Go, tell it on the mountain
> That Jesus Christ is born
>
> While shepherds kept their watching
> Over silent flocks by night
> Behold, throughout the heavens
> There shone a holy light
>
> Go, tell it on the mountain
> Over the hills and everywhere
> Go, tell it on the mountain
> That Jesus Christ is born
>
> The shepherds feared and trembled
> When lo! above the earth
> Rang out the angels' chorus
> That hailed the Savior's birth
>
> Go, tell it on the mountain
> Over the hills and everywhere
> Go, tell it on the mountain
> That Jesus Christ is born

Of interest in this song is the citing of the shepherds, a powerful biblical imagery of the systemically marginalized, like young David, being acknowledged and elevated to a new-life status of inclusion. In my lifelong experiences with Black church nativity dramatizations, Mary is never the one admonishing the oppressed to spread the good news of new life in oppressive contexts. It is done by the supporting cast who witnessed the Christ event. The witnessing audience is invited to join the cast in proclaiming the good news "over the hills and everywhere." Again, Mary is silent, but her role as the vessel for incarnation is an implicit backdrop to the narrative.

In African American sermons and reenactments, her lowly status and faithfulness are sometimes highlighted to draw parallels with the experiences of enslaved or impoverished mothers. Mary's role in the Christmas story affirmed that God works through the marginalized and that African American mothers, often dismissed or dehumanized, share in her sacred dignity. Since Christmas traditionally brings hopeful glad tidings, singing this song was the highlight of dramatic presentations or sermons and inspired struck-low people to go forth with emboldened faith.

Jesus's crucifixion illuminates Mary's faithfulness in spirituals such as *Were You There When They Crucified My Lord?* I vividly recall the late Reverend Dr. Manuel Scott, Sr., sermonically riveting us with an emotional interpretation of this song. He used the song as a cultural artifact, or perhaps a poetic transporter, prompting us to join Mary at the crucifixion. As powerful as that sermonic moment was, Mary remained silent throughout the traumatizing ordeal of her son's brutal lynching. While not always naming Mary directly, the lamentation within the song reflects her grief as she stood by the cross, bearing witness to her son's unjust death. For African Americans, particularly during slavery and the lynching era, Mary's sorrow mirrored their own experiences of hopelessly standing by and watching loved ones suffer, being sold, and too often dying a cruel death at the hands of systemic violence. Mary symbolized shared pain and resilience in the face of brutal injustices.

Certainly, African American art and gospel music have often depicted Mary as a maternal figure of strength and compassion. Gospel songs like *Sweet Little Jesus Boy*, as sung by Mahalia Jackson, indirectly reference Mary's care for the infant Jesus while reflecting on racial suffering and redemption themes.

> Sweet little Jesus boy
> They made you be born in a manger
> Sweet little holy child
> We didn't know who you were
> Didn't know you'd come to save us, Lord
> To take our sins away
> Our eyes were blind; we could not see
> We didn't know who you were
>
> Long time ago
> You were born
> Born in a manger, Lord
> Sweet little Jesus boy
> The world treats you mean, Lord
> Treats me mean, too
> But that's how things are down here
> We don't know who you are

Again, Mary's voice is implied, and the existential connections are quite clear. These cultural representations allowed African Americans to see Mary as a symbol of divine love and solidarity while embodying the nurturing care and resilience of Black motherhood. Please note that in *Sweet Little Jesus Boy*, Jesus's humanity is not magnified even while cloaked in infancy. His divinity and ministry purpose rob him of a childhood. Yet, it is his humanity that connects with the humanity of Black people, whose full personhood has long been ignored and minimized throughout the American experience. He is not known, nor are we known.

I include Whitney Houston's stirring nativity song, *Who Could Imagine*, because of its cultural value in contemporary Black life. While it does not appeal to traditional nativity themes and sensitivities, it anchors itself in modern Black motherhood struggles to dare envision greatness in every Black child. This song highlights the mystery of the incarnation, where God uses the common birth of a child as a prop for divine purpose.

Mommies and daddies always believe
That their little angels are special indeed
And you could grow up to be anything
But who would imagine a king?

A shepherd or teacher is what you could be
Or maybe a fisherman out on the sea
Or maybe a carpenter building things
But who would imagine a king?

It was so clear when the wise men arrived
And the angels were singing your name
That the world would be different 'cause you were alive
That's what heaven stood still to proclaim

One day, an angel said quietly
That soon he would bring something special to me
And of all those wonderful gifts he could bring

Who would imagine, who could imagine
Who would imagine a king?

Here is a song that was not a part of my introduction to Mary, yet it speaks to the creativity of the once-enslaved. Of interest in this song is the prominence of Joseph in a song about Mary as the Queen of Galilee.

The Cherry Tree Carol
From the Ritchie family of Kentucky.

When Joseph was an old man,
An old man was he,
He married the Virgin Mary,
The Queen of Galilee.

He married the Virgin Mary,
The Queen of Galilee.

As Joseph and Mary
Walked through an orchard good,
Here are apples and cherries
As red as any blood.

As Joseph and Mary
Walked through an orchard green,
Here are apples and cherries
As thick as might be seen.
Then up spoke sweet Mary,
So meek and so mild,
"Joseph, gather me some cherries,
For I am with child."

Then Joseph flew in angry,
In angry flew he,
"Let the father of the baby
Gather cherries for thee."

Then up spoke sweet Jesus,
All in his mother's womb,
"Bow down, you tallest tree,
That my mother might have some."

So low bowed that cherry tree,
Down low to the ground,
And Mary gathered cherries
While Joseph stood around.

Then Joseph took Mary
All on his left knee,
Said, "Tell me, pretty baby,
When your birthday will be."

"On the sixth day of January

My birthday will be.

When the stars and the elements

Shall tremble with glee."

Another intriguing artifact from black culture is the dramatic play, *Black Nativity*. Langston Hughes discerned the diminished role of Mary in our telling of the story and our singing about it. He noted that spirituals "based on the birth or infancy of Jesus" were "extremely rare." He speculated that the "Negro preferred to think of Jesus as God, as almighty, all-powerful to help" (Hughes, 1926, p. 14). Furthermore, Hughes observed that Christ's birth was not a particularly sacred or religious observance in the South, but a time of celebration with "gunpowder and whiskey, singing, dancing, visiting; to guzzling, gluttony, and debauchery" (Hughes, 1926, pp. 14–15).

Black Nativity was first performed in 1961, among a complexity of cultural concerns, understandably among whites, but surprisingly so for Blacks. It is a unique retelling of the Nativity story, blending the traditional Christian narrative of the birth of Jesus with elements of African American culture and spiritual expression. Reportedly, one performer, an African American, Carmen De Lavallade, a star dancer with the Metropolitan Opera, was offended by the title. "The title seems in bad taste, and I don't want to be a part of it," she explained, as she stormed off the set and left the cast along with her loyal friend and colleague, Alvin Ailey."[9]

As a testament to his faith and commitment to Black life and art, Langston Hughes set the Nativity story in the context of the African American experience. The production featured a predominantly Black cast and incorporated gospel music, spirituals, and cultural references that resonate with the Black community. Central characters like Mary and Joseph embodied both the struggle and the faith of African Americans. The play highlighted the themes of hope, resilience, and the enduring power of faith amidst adversity.

Hughes used the setting of Harlem to frame the story, making it a celebration of Black culture while maintaining the sacredness of the Christmas narrative. The extensive use of music was integral, with soulful arrangements that reflected both joy and sorrow, capturing the essence of the Black church tradition. The characters' interactions and the portrayal of the Holy Family connected deeply with the struggles faced by African Americans, drawing parallels between the oppression of the biblical characters and the contemporary struggle for civil rights.

Hughes wrote *Black Nativity* to provide a voice for African Americans within the Christian tradition. He aimed to reclaim and reinterpret the Nativity story through a lens that reflects the African

---

9   Arnold Rampersad, "The Life of Langston Hughes, Volume 2, (Oxford University Press, Inc., New York, New York, 1988), p 341

American experience. By doing so, he sought to affirm the dignity, strength, and faith of Black people, especially during a time when they faced systemic racism and social injustice in America.

He believed art should serve as a medium for social change and community empowerment. He wanted to challenge the dominant narratives that often marginalized or overlooked Black voices in religious contexts. *Black Nativity* emerged as a powerful statement of identity, faith, and cultural pride, inviting audiences to see the Christmas story in a new light—one that celebrates Black heritage and emphasizes the universal themes of love, hope, and redemption. He used the performing arts to give voice to black pain and love, life, and struggle.

Interestingly, in *Black Nativity*, Mary's character held a central role that was both poignant and powerful. She embodied themes of faith, resilience, and the struggles faced by Black women, particularly within the context of her circumstances as an unwed mother in a historical and social landscape that is laden with social challenges. Mary was portrayed as a deeply faithful figure, embodying trust in God's plan despite the societal stigma surrounding her pregnancy. Her acceptance of the divine message reflects a profound spiritual strength, as she navigates her journey with grace and determination. This faith is especially resonant given the historical context of the African American community, where faith has been a cornerstone of resilience in the face of oppression.

In *Black Nativity*, Mary's character represents the complexity of Black womanhood, symbolizing strength and vulnerability. Hughes captures her inner struggles, portraying her not just as the mother of Jesus but as a Black woman facing the trials of poverty, discrimination, and societal judgment. This duality highlights her as a relatable figure for many African American women, who often juggle similar societal pressures.

Mary's character also reflects the broader struggles against systemic oppression. Her journey to bring forth Jesus can be seen as a metaphor for the community's fight to bring forth justice and dignity. Hughes contextualized Mary within the African American experience, linking her trials with those of the community and showcasing her as a beacon of hope. In a stroke of artistic genius, Hughes used Mary's story as a literary midwife for Black hope being birthed despite the dehumanizing brutalities of white oppression.

Unlike some traditional portrayals, where Mary is blandly meek and mild, Hughes gave Mary rich emotional depth and agency. She emotively grappled with her fears and uncertainties while also demonstrating strength and leadership. This portrayal allowed Mary to take an active role in her narrative, making choices that emphasize her agency as a mother and as a faithful participant in the divine plan. Through Mary, Hughes connected the Nativity story to African American cultural elements, infusing it with spiritual songs and rhythms that reflect the community's heritage. This cultural significance enhanced the emotional resonance of her character with the Black community and emphasized the importance of cultural identity in the expression of faith.

In concert with the biblical portrayal, Mary served as a symbol of perseverance, demonstrating how faith can guide one through adversity and uncertainty. Her journey was central to the narrative, emphasizing the love and sacrifice involved in nurturing the divine child. The portrayal of Mary in *Black Nativity* offers a nuanced interpretation that both aligns with and diverges from the traditional perspective of Mary in Black churches.

Hear again this Christmas story -

Christ is born in all His glory.

Baby laid in manger dark,

Lighting ages with the spark

Of innocence that is the Child,

Trusting all within His smile.

Tell again the Christmas story

With the halo of His glory;

Halo born of humbleness

By the breath of cattle blest,

By the poverty of stall

Where a bed of straw is all,

By a door closed at the Inn

Where only men of means get in,

By a door closed to the poor.

Christ is born on earthen floor

In a stable with no lock-

Yet kingdoms tremble at the shock

Of a King in swaddling clothes

At an address no one knows

Because there is no hotel sign -

Nothing but a star divine,

Nothing but a halo bright

About His young head in the night.

Mary's Son in manger born!

Music of the Angel's horn!

Mary's Son in straw and glory!

Wonder of the Christmas story!

Langston Hughes

DISCUSSION QUESTIONS

1. Do you have a favorite song about Mary? What is it?

2. Which Mary did you associate the song, *O Mary Don't You Weep* with?

3. Have you ever seen or read Langston Hughes's play *Black Nativity*? If so, what were your impressions of Mary?

4. How has Mary shown up in the cultural artifacts of your church and/or community?

Chapter 3

OH MARY, DON'T YOU WEEP PT: 2

MARIOLOGY EXAMINED

"I am Mary. I am not another woman's life, nor
is her life mine.
My life is in God's hands. I am open to
God's divine imagination.
I am open to my own possibilities.
Don't confuse me with your low expectations for me.
Don't torture me with your needs.
Don't blind me by reminding me where I came from.
I have communed with angels.
There's more to me than meets the eye.
My name is Mary. And I am pregnant with unnamed possibilities.
(Weems, 2002, pp. 35-36)

Mary might have cause to weep if she saw how Western and Black theology minimized her in contrast to the Latin American Liberation theologians who have dramatically illuminated her. Western theology, consistent with its patriarchal proclivities and class privileges, acknowledges Mary but never tries to include her or magnify her voice or grant her soteriological significance. Traditionally, Mariology is a theological category that focuses its discussions on Mary, the mother of Jesus. It seeks to connect the doctrines or dogmas concerning Mary to other doctrines of the faith, such as those related to Jesus and notions about redemption, intercession, and grace. Catholicism has held a larger space for the branch of theology that studies the life and prerogatives of the "Blessed Virgin" and provides her a perfunctory place in the economy of salvation and sanctification. [Alvin] I use the following discussion on Mary to substantiate what I believe is helpful, particularly when theologically considering Mary in Catholicism and Protestantism.

MARY IN CATHOLICISM

[Alvin] My introduction to Catholicism began in childhood, during interactions with Catholic families in the neighborhood. I played with Black Catholic boys and admired the beauty of the Black Catholic girls. The few Black Catholic families in my community exuded a sense of "Black privilege," often textured with lighter skin. They attended Catholic schools, wore distinct uniforms, and attended Catholic mass. Their parents associated with other Catholic parents and were kind but noticeably standoffish toward their Protestant neighbors and children. However, their struggles with Blackness reduced many of my Catholic peers into the same dark holes of despair as the rest of us. I witnessed both the young men and women struggle with black life in America, just like the rest of us. Racism was not kind to Black Catholics or Black Protestants. While they may have carried rosary beads, I never heard any of my Black Catholic friends cry out to Mary in the midst of Black suffering. I am certain they knew the Mariological litanies, but I never witnessed them turning to those devotions as they painfully grappled with the challenges of blackness in East Oakland, California. Depressant drugs were more common among my Black Catholic friends.

[Diana] I grew up Baptist in East Oakland during the 1950s and 1960s. In my church, Mary was mentioned only in Christmas plays or in passing during the nativity story. She was never lifted up as a voice to be studied, or a presence with something to say to our lives.

I knew a few folks from the neighborhood who went to Catholic school. To us Baptist kids, they seemed kind of bougie—dressed in their uniforms, carrying themselves with a sense of difference. Their families went to mass while we stayed with our Sunday choirs and Baptist shout. From the outside looking in, I knew they had rosaries, novenas, and prayers that mentioned Mary, but none of that spilled into the streets of East Oakland where racism, poverty, and struggle pressed on us all.

Mary didn't show up in my Baptist world, and she didn't seem to show up in my Catholic neighbors' world either—not when it came to the lived pain of Black life. She was muted in both places, hidden by patriarchy on one side and ritual distance on the other.

Interesting, because in Catholicism, Mariology is rich and complex, deeply intertwined with the Church's doctrines, liturgy, and popular devotion. For instance, Mariology in the Catholic church is constructed around six primary tenets, which I briefly eplain. This section is mildly academic but necessary for a wholesome understanding of Mary. I keep the explanations brief and accessible. If you want to know more, refer to the theological dictionaries.

The primary tenets of Mariology are: (a) Mary as Theotokos (Mother of God), (b) Immaculate Conception, (c) Perpetual Virginity, (d) Assumption, (e) Co-Redemptrix and Mediatrix, and (f) Devotional Practices. I offer abbreviated introductions to each with concise definitions and reflections on their theological meaning, offered not for argument, but for awareness and insight.

1. **Mary as Theotokos (Mother of God)**
   - **Definition**: Affirmed at the Council of Ephesus (431), Mary is venerated as the *Theotokos* (God-bearer), emphasizing her role as the mother of Jesus, who is fully God and fully human.
   - **Theological Significance:** For the Catholics, this title safeguards the doctrine of the Incarna-

tion, affirming that Jesus' divinity and humanity are united.

2. **Immaculate Conception**

   - **Definition**: Proclaimed as dogma by Pope Pius IX in 1854, this teaching holds that Mary was conceived without original sin to prepare her to be the mother of Jesus.

   - **Theological Significance**: This doctrine interestingly highlights God's grace and Mary's unique role in salvation history.

3. **Perpetual Virginity**

   - **Definition:** The belief that Mary remained a virgin before, during, and after the birth of Jesus.

   - **Theological Significance**: This position reinforces her purity and complete dedication to God.

4. **Assumption**

   - **Definition:** Declared dogma in 1950 by Pope Pius XII, this teaching holds that Mary was assumed body and soul into heaven at the end of her earthly life.

   - **Theological Significance**: It reflects Mary's role as the first to fully experience the resurrection and glorification promised to all believers.

5. **Co-Redemptrix and Mediatrix**

   - **Definition:** While not dogma, Mary is sometimes referred to as Co-Redemptrix, emphasizing her cooperation in Jesus' redemptive work, and Mediatrix, highlighting her role in interceding for humanity.

   - **Theological Significance:** As such it emphasizes Mary's ongoing spiritual motherhood and intercessory role.

6. **Devotional Practices**

   - **Examples:** Prayers such as the *Hail Mary*, the Rosary, and Marian feasts emphasize her importance in Catholic spirituality.

MARY IN PROTESTANTISM

I am certain that no Protestants in my church circle ever cried out to Mary, carried rosary beads, or considered her much beyond Christmas pageantry. I have observed a few small pictures and Mary figurines strategically placed in some homes. Curiosity prompted me to journey outside the liturgical walls of my Protestant silo, and I discovered that for Protestants, Mariology is far more limited, reflecting the Reformation's emphasis on *sola scriptura* (Scripture alone) and the rejection of practices commonly seen as unbiblical. Essentially, in Protestantism, we find the following:

1. **Mary as Theotokos**

- **Definition:** Protestants closely connected to Catholicism, such as Episcopalians and Presbyterians, accept Mary as the Mother of God based on the Christological significance affirmed at the Council of Ephesus. However, she remains a minor stand-alone character in the Christ story. She is honored for her role in the Incarnation but not venerated.

2. **Rejection of the Immaculate Conception**
   - Protestants generally reject this doctrine as lacking explicit biblical support and undermining the universality of sin and grace.

3. **Virgin Birth (but not Perpetual Virginity)**
   - Protestants affirm Mary's virginity at Jesus' conception and birth, but many do not hold that she remained a virgin afterward. Much of this resistance is based in Western cultures' issues with human sexuality, discussed earlier. This position, however, aligns with biblical accounts but avoids elevating Mary beyond her scriptural role.

4. **Mary as a Model of Faith**
   - Protestants view Mary as a model of faith and obedience, particularly in her "yes" to God at the Annunciation (Luke 1:38). Mary exemplifies trust in God's promises, making her a relatable figure of discipleship.

5. **Rejection of Marian Devotions**
   - Marian prayers and devotions are rejected as unnecessary or idolatrous, based on the belief that Christ is the sole mediator (1 Timothy 2:5). This position preserves the Protestant emphasis on direct access to God through Christ.

Some Key Differences in Catholicism and Protestantism

1. **Nature of Veneration:**
   - **Catholics:** Mary is venerated (*hyperdulia*), not worshipped, as uniquely graced by God.
   - **Protestants:** Mary is honored but not venerated to avoid detracting from Christ.

2. **Role in Salvation:**
   - **Catholics:** Mary is seen as actively participating in salvation history.
   - **Protestants:** Mary is viewed as a passive recipient of God's grace, with no co-redemptive role.

3. **Sources of Authority:**
   - **Catholics:** Teachings are derived from Scripture, tradition, and Magisterial authority.
   - **Protestants:** Teachings about Mary are limited to direct biblical references.

Conclusion

Catholic Mariology elevates Mary as a central figure in salvation history and a model of grace, while Protestant traditions regard her as an important but secondary figure to Christ. These theological frameworks influence the practices, devotions, and understanding of Mary's role in Christian life and thought. Protestantism, on the other hand, supports the Apostles' Creed, affirming the virgin birth of Christ while largely rejecting its other tenets of Mariology. Protestants denounce the veneration of Mary as practiced by Roman Catholicism and Eastern Orthodoxy.

MARY IN THE APOSTLE'S CREED

I believe in God, the Father Almighty,

The Creator of heaven and earth,

and in Jesus Christ, His only Son, our Lord:

Who was conceived of the Holy Spirit,

born of the Virgin Mary,

suffered under Pontius Pilate,

was crucified, died, and was buried.

MARY HAD A BABY

Black Theology Matters

Mary had a baby, my Lord.

What did she name him, my Lord?

She named him King Jesus, my Lord.

Where was he born, my Lord?

Born in a manger, my Lord.

~ Author Unknown

Undeniably, Black theology provides much to the witnessing capacity of the Black church. However, it should be noted that Black academicians, as articulate and "special" as many delusionally presume, did not create Black theology because academics did not make the Black church. Like Jesus, who asserted, "Before Abraham was, I am," before Black theology was, the Black church "is." Moreover, like Jesus, the Black church is God's creative response to a dominating evil imposed upon an oppressed and dehumanized people. The Black church and its people's experiences, social contexts, and culture provide the necessary resources for crafting Black theology. Without the Black church and the lived experiences of Black people, Black theology would be neither relevant nor helpful.

Traditionally, Western theology has drawn from four primary sources: scripture, tradition, reasoning, and human experience. Alistar E. McGrath (2011) noted that these "four main sources have been acknowledged within the Christian tradition."[10]

---

10 Alistar E. McGrath, Christian Theology: An Introduction, (John Wiley & Sons Ltd., Chichester, West Sussex, 2017), p. 104

- **Scripture** – The sacred texts, primarily the Bible, regarded as authoritative for faith and practice. The Bible serves as a foundation for understanding God and God's intent/will.

- **Tradition** – The collective teachings, practices, and interpretations of the Church throughout history. Tradition holds powerful influences over doctrinal development and communal life.

- **Reasoning** – The use of logical and philosophical inquiry to understand and construct theological concepts. This a uniquely Western thought process that seeks to reconcile faith with rational thought and explore ethical implications.

- **Religious experience** – The personal and communal experiences of believers that inform their understanding of God and faith, often leading to insights and new understandings.

However, Black Theology, as constructed by James Cone, added to the theological query, citing Biblical history and Black liberation as essential sources.[11] Those essential sources that distinguish themselves from traditional theology, succinctly defined, are:

- **Black History** – The biblical witness of God's involvement in history as being actively involved in the liberation of the oppressed.

- **Black Liberation** – It involves taking seriously the necessity of making the Christian message relevant to our time; thus, we conclude that Christian theology in America must be Black.[12]

Black theology matters because all traditional sources of theology are rethought and reimagined through the broad lens of the Black experience. One of Black theology's great contributions is its systematized criticism of Western theology's many racist and bigoted assumptions. In Black theology, oppressive constructs and ideologies embedded within Western theology are critiqued, condemned, and reformatted to address the Black experience.

Black theology has played a vital role in amplifying the voices of Black individuals. However, it has mainly focused on addressing the theological gaps present in predominantly white-male Protestantism. In doing so, Black theology has developed its own blind spots in response to these issues. Just as Protestants tended to ignore Mary's role in the drama of salvation history, Black theology likewise minimized her standing in Christian culture. For instance, in America, many Protestant churches are named St. Andrew's, St. Mark's, and St. Stephen's, but rarely is one found named St. Mary's. Having lived in various populous communities from the West Coast, South, and East Coast, I know of no Mother Mary United Methodist Church, a Saint Mary Baptist Church, or a Mary District Association. However, by any objective analysis, Mary plays a far more critical role in biblical accounts than Andrew, Mark, or Stephen.

---

11   James H. Cone & Gayraud S. Wilmore, Black Theology: A Documentary History, volume 1:1966-1979, (Orbis Books, Maryknoll, New York, 1993), pp.110-111. The citing of the two essential sources of Biblical History and Black Liberation reflects a shift in his earlier writing in 1970, where he cites six sources: 1. Black Experience, 2. Black History, 3. Black Culture, 4. Revelation,5. Scripture, 6. Reasoning A Black Theology of Liberation, (Orbis Books, Mary Knoll, New York, 1970) pp. 24-33.

12   Ibid., p. 112

The church of my youth was Bethlehem Missionary Baptist and the New Nazarene Missionary Baptist. In Dallas, I worshipped at the Northpark Baptist Church; in Nashville, I served at Olivet Baptist Church; and in Brooklyn, at Mount Lebanon Baptist Church. All were named after towns or communities. Although geographically and socially significant, none carry nearly the same theologically or emotionally significant meaning as Mary. It appears that even black people would rather name a church after a city, or a theological concept than to name one after a woman, even a person as biblically significant as Mary.

[Diana] Even as a young girl, though I didn't have the language yet, I sensed that absence. Later, through the lens of Womanist theology, I came to recognize what I was feeling: that Mary's silence was part of a larger pattern, the way women's voices and experiences were diminished in both Protestant and Catholic spaces. Womanist theologians have taught us that when women's voices are absent, something holy is missing. Looking back, I realize that in all the prayers and preaching of my youth, Mary should have been standing there with us, testifying to survival and hope in the middle of East Oakland. But her voice was muted, like so many of our mothers, aunties, and grandmothers.

And yet, there was one place where I *did* hear women's voices: the beauty shop. Under the hiss of the hot comb, women told the truth—about betrayal, about joy, about the grit it took to raise children in hard times. They poured out theology without calling it that. They testified without a pulpit. It makes me wonder now: what if the church had listened to the women in the salon as carefully as it listened to the men in the pulpit? What if we had heard Mary's Magnificat the way we heard women humming while waiting for their hair to set—honest, defiant, and unashamed?

THE PROTESTANT ROOTS OF BLACK THEOLOGY

As previously stated, Black theology emerged primarily within the African American Protestant tradition, shaped by the historical legacy of the Black church. Protestantism, particularly in its American expression, tends to downplay Mary's role in theology due to several factors:

1. **Reformation Theology**: The Protestant Reformation rejected what reformers saw as the over-emphasis on Mary in Catholic theology. They reduced Mary's role to that of a faithful servant and de-emphasized Marian doctrines like her perpetual virginity, immaculate conception, and assumption. These theological shifts influenced the way many Black Protestant churches conceptualized Mary.

2. **Sola Scriptura Emphasis**: Protestant reliance on *sola scriptura* (Scripture alone) often led to a focus on texts explicitly centered on Jesus' ministry and mission, leaving less room for extensive reflection on Mary's role in salvation history. In this regard, Black Theology, for the most part, retained its biblical roots.

3. **Low Ecclesiology**: Protestantism's tendency to downplay hierarchical structures and saintly intercession further diminished Mary's presence, as Protestants generally rejected her role as an intercessor. This Protestant heritage strongly shaped Black Theology's development, but silencing and leaving Mary largely absent from its framework.

A Perspective on Christocentric Liberation

Black Theology, as articulated by figures like James Cone and Gayruad S. Wilmore, centers Jesus Christ as the primary symbol of liberation for oppressed peoples. This Christocentric emphasis emerged in response to systemic racism, white supremacy, and the need for a theology that affirms Black identity and dignity. Nevertheless, in a subtle, perhaps unintended way, it sustained patriarchy and the distortions of individualism. I understand why Black Theology emphasized **Jesus as the Liberator**. Within this framework, Jesus is understood as the figure who identifies with the oppressed, particularly in his crucifixion and resurrection. However, the exclusive focus on Jesus as the suffering, liberating Savior often overshadows other biblical figures, including Mary, who are pivotal to the narrative of salvation. Jesus was part of a community; the community shaped who he was and provided context to his ministry. Yet the **Christological priority** in liberation theology in the African American context has prioritized Christology (the study of Christ) over Mariology (the study of Mary), partly because Jesus' life and death are seen as direct models for confronting oppression and systemic injustice. I leave it to the scholars and the unfolding revelations of history to sort out and clarify the negligence and oversights of Black theology.

I understand and appreciate that **social relevance** precipitated addressing urgent social issues like slavery, segregation, and police violence. Black theologians leaned heavily on Jesus as a figure of radical solidarity and hope, leaving less space for exploring Mary's potential contributions to liberation. Unfortunately, Black theology's reactions to Western Christianity inadvertently aligned itself with Eurocentric Marian devotion by silencing Mary. In doing so, it skimmed over the blackness in the drama of Mary.

OUT OF TOUCH WITH MARY

Historically, Marian devotion has been shaped by European cultural and aesthetic norms, which have often felt alien to African American spiritual and cultural traditions. One major obstacle was the colonial legacy of Marian imagery. In Western Christianity, the dominant visual images of Mary are depicted as a European woman. Such a presentation reinforced a sense of cultural distance, presenting a Mary who is out of touch with Black life. I was aesthetically overwhelmed by this reality during a recent tour of the Louvre Museum in Paris, France. It seemed as if all great European artists had produced a painting of Mary in white imagery, with no regard for other cultural expressions. This imagery often fails to resonate with African American experiences, which are deeply rooted in a history of cultural survival and resistance against colonial and white supremacist narratives.

There was also a cultural disconnect within African American contexts. European portrayals of Mary emphasized her as a symbol of purity, obedience, and submission, traits that conflicted with the image of agency and resistance central to liberation theology. This disconnect discouraged theological engagement with Mary in black religious spaces. While visiting Detroit, my host and friend, Edward L. Branch, took me on a tour that included visiting the Shrine of the Black Madonna. I had read Albert Cleage's work and was excited to have an opportunity to visit and learn how the Black Madonna organizationally functioned within the church (Cleage, 1968). I was largely disappointed. Cleage's veneration of the Black Madonna—a powerful symbolic reclaiming of Black feminine divinity— suggested at first glance a liberative, woman-centered theology. However, beneath the iconography, the internal structure, culture, and theological underpinnings of the *Shrine of the Black Madonna* were deeply patriarchal, reflecting many of the same gendered hierarchies that pervaded both traditional Black churches and Black nationalist movements of the 20th century. Moreover, the intellectual acuity needed to embrace Cleage's theology proved challenging to the average Detroit church goer, whose faith was largely shaped by the emotional expressions of traditional Black religion.

There were no Black Madonna presentations in the churches of my community. Only when a black woman or black child played the part of Mary during the once-a-year Christmas program was she ever black. A once-a-year image hardly erases the cultural disconnect experienced from a lifetime of white Marys, coupled with a lifetime of white Jesus. While Marian devotions in Latin America and Africa have contextualized Mary as a figure of liberation (e.g., *Our Lady of Guadalupe* and *Our Lady of Aparecida*), such models have not historically been integrated into African American religious life.

MOVING FROM MARY-LITE

Perhaps Mary's role in Black theology was minimized due to Black theology's historical and theological priorities focused on survival and justice in the face of systemic oppression. Black theology developed as a response to the pressing needs of the African American community, addressing slavery, segregation, economic injustice, and police brutality. These urgent concerns have often taken precedence over theological exploration of figures like Mary, and we might even add Joseph, Zechariah, Elizabeth, Simeon, Anna, and the rest of Jesus's community. Addressing the daunting challenges of a legacy of oppression prompted a theology heavily reliant on the prophetic ministry of Jesus, but "lite" on the significance of Mary.

Admittedly, early Black theology was predominantly male-dominated, with limited attention to the experiences and contributions of women. As a result, figures like Mary, who hold particular relevance for Womanist theology, were largely ignored. Many Black Protestant theologians rejected traditional Marian doctrines (e.g., immaculate conception and intercessory role) as unnecessary or unbiblical, further limiting their engagement with Mary as a theological figure.

However, recent developments in Womanist and Afrocentric theologies have begun to address this gap, exploring Mary as a figure of resilience, motherhood, and liberation. Womanist theologians such as Delores S. Williams and Emilie Townes have pointed to the importance of maternal and feminine imagery in theological reflection, opening new avenues for Marian engagement in Black theology (Townes, 1995; Williams, 1993). Williams defines the landscape of womanist theology when she states:

Womanist theology attempt to help black women see, affirm, and have confidence in the importance of their experience and faith for determining the character of the Christian religion in the African American community. Womanist theology challenges all oppressive forces impeding black women's struggle for survival and for the development of a positive productive quality of life conducive to women's and the family's freedom and well-being. Womanist theology opposes all oppression based on race, sex, class, sexual preference, physical disability and caste."[13]

While I believe her to be a staunch womanist, Rachel St. Claire's Christological focus in *True to Our Native Land* (2007) overlooks serious Marian engagement. I understand Jesus being her primary concern, but even God uses Mary to get Jesus in the world. As previously stated, Dr. Mitzi Smith has hermeneutically upset traditional interpretations of Mary with her *doule* perspective. She provides a hermeneutical off ramp for all who want to embrace a serious Black Mariology.

MARY IN LATIN AMERICAN LIBERATION THEOLOGY

We find it theologically fascinating that Mary, the mother of Jesus, occupies a central role in South American liberation theology as a symbol of hope, solidarity with the poor, and a powerful model for social and political resistance against oppression. Her presence is interpreted through the lens of the *preferential option for the poor*, a foundational principle of liberation theology that emphasizes God's particular concern for the marginalized.

Mary as the Model of the Poor and Oppressed

Mary is often portrayed as a poor, young woman living under Roman occupation, embodying the realities faced by many in Latin America. Her *Magnificat* (Luke 1:46-55) is a cornerstone text in Latin liberation theology, interpreted as a radical hymn of justice, expressing God's intervention in overturning oppressive structures. The passage emphasizes God's lifting up of the lowly and filling the hungry, directly addressing themes of socioeconomic inequality. Gustavo Gutiérrez, often considered the father of liberation theology, emphasizes that Mary's life reflects God's solidarity with the poor. She stands as a figure who listens to the cries of the oppressed and responds with a prophetic vision of justice, symbolizing the active participation of the faithful in challenging systemic injustice.

Mary as the Maternal Protector

In many South American communities, Mary is also revered as a maternal figure who offers comfort and protection to the poor and suffering. Devotions to Mary, particularly under the symbols of

---

13 Delores Williams, Sisters in the Wilderness: The Challenge of Womanist God-Talk (Orbis Books, Maryknoll, N.Y.) xiv.

Our Lady of Guadalupe, *Our Lady of Aparecida*, and *Our Lady of Sorrows*, highlight her identification with indigenous and Afro-descendant populations. These titles symbolize her presence among marginalized groups and her intercession in their struggles for justice. For example, *Our Lady of Guadalupe* is celebrated as an advocate for the indigenous peoples of Mexico and beyond, representing their dignity and humanity in the face of colonial oppression. Similarly, *Our Lady of Aparecida*, the patroness of Brazil, is seen as a unifying figure who calls for liberation and inclusion.

OUR LADY OF GUADALUPE – Mexico

https://en.wikipedia.org/wiki/Our_Lady_of_Guadalupe

Our Lady of Guadalupe is an iconic representation of Mary, based on the apparitions to Saint Juan Diego, an indigenous man, in 1531 near Mexico City. The image of the Virgin imprinted on Juan Diego's tilma (cloak) features Mary with brown skin, indigenous facial features, and surrounded by symbols resonant with Mesoamerican cosmology. Her theological significance plants her in solidarity with the marginalized. *Our Lady of Guadalupe* embodies solidarity with indigenous and oppressed peoples, challenging colonial and racial hierarchies. She is seen as a liberator who identifies with the suffering of the poor and the colonized. Her imagery blends Catholic Marian devotion with indigenous symbols, such as the tilma and the stars on her mantle, making Christianity accessible and affirming indigenous culture within the faith.

Within liberation theology, she is regarded as a revolutionary figure who fosters resistance against oppression and colonialism. She symbolizes God's preferential option for the poor, as she appeared to an Indigenous peasant rather than the Spanish elite. Also, during Latin America's revolutionary movements, Guadalupe became a symbol for peasant uprisings and labor movements, inspiring hope and a call to action against systemic injustices.

OUR LADY OF APARECIDA - Brazil

Our Lady of Aparecida, the patroness of Brazil, originated from the miraculous discovery of a small clay statue by fishermen in 1717 in the Paraíba River. After the statue's recovery, a series of miracles were attributed to her intercession, leading to her veneration. She is the Black Madonna of Aparecida in Brazilian Liberation Theology. The Black Madonna of Aparecida, known as *Nossa Senhora Aparecida*, is the patroness of Brazil and one of the most significant Marian icons in Latin America. According to the tradition, the fishermen, struggling to catch fish, prayed for divine assistance. After finding the statue, their nets became miraculously full, which they instinctively knew had not come from the Brazilian elites or Portuguese colonizers. They knew God had intervened and made a definitive commitment to the poor and oppressed. This miraculous event sparked devotion to *Our Lady of Aparecida*, and her significance has grown, especially among Brazil's marginalized populations.

The witness of the poor fishermen propelled Aparecida's story and underscores God's intervention and care for the downtrodden. Her image as a Black Madonna resonates deeply with Afro-Brazilian communities, symbolizing divine solidarity with those facing racial and economic oppression. Of interest is the statue's dark skin, which challenges Eurocentric depictions of Mary and Christianity, affirming the dignity and spiritual significance of Blackness within a Brazilian context shaped by colonialism and slavery. As a Black Madonna, she stands as a counter-narrative to the colonial imposition of a white, European-centered Christianity. This resonates with liberation theology's goal of contextualizing faith within the lived realities of marginalized communities.

While the huge Euro-featured statue of Christ the Redeemer looms large in contemporary Brazilian art and tourism, Aparecida serves a role in community mobilization. For instance, the annual pilgrimage to the Basilica of Aparecida is a site of pilgrimage for millions, often becoming a space for collective reflection on social justice. During political upheavals, her image has been invoked in calls for equity and human rights. Aparecida is revered not only in Catholicism but also among practitioners of Afro-Brazilian traditions, symbolizing a bridge between Catholic faith and African heritage. This dual veneration enhances her role as a unifying figure in social justice movements.

In my travels worldwide, Brazil stands out as one of my most memorable. Despite the glaring economic inequities, it is an amazing country with incredibly beautiful people. Yet, it is in this country where some of the most thoughtful social and theological responses to colonized oppression emerge. The use of the Black Madonna of Aparecida continues to inform and inspire. For instance, in 2007, the *Fifth General Conference of Latin American Bishops* (CELAM), held at Aparecida, emphasized a renewed commitment to the preferential option for the poor. Held under the patronage of *Our Lady of Aparecida*, this conference solidified her as a theological and spiritual symbol of liberation. The bishops invoked her story to inspire pastoral action focused on addressing systemic injustice and poverty.

Today, Aparecida continues to serve as a source of hope for Brazil's marginalized communities, particularly women and Afro-Brazilian populations. Her presence serves as a reminder of divine accompaniment in their struggles for equality and dignity. Afro-Brazilian activists have invoked Aparecida to highlight the intersection of faith and racial equity, using her image to challenge systemic racism within both church and society.

OUR LADY OF SORROW - *Argentina*

Argentina stands out as another of my memorable travel experiences. Throughout the country, many of the inequities of colonization remain unanswered by the provocations of liberation theology. Among those provocations stands *Our Lady of Sorrow* in La Plata, Argentina, who artistically identifies with the lingering trauma suffered by the oppressed.

Our Lady of Sorrows depicts Mary as the grieving mother, pierced by seven swords, each representing the sorrows she endured, including the crucifixion of her son. This imagery often portrays Mary in mourning, emphasizing her solidarity with human suffering. She is a maternal figure who understands and shares in the suffering of humanity. She provides comfort and hope to those enduring systemic violence and personal loss. Throughout Latin America, she resonates particularly with mothers who have lost children to political violence, femicide, or poverty, embodying their pain and struggle for justice. Liberation theologians use her as a model for standing alongside the afflicted and advocating for justice. The mothers of the disappeared in Argentina (*Las Madres de Plaza de Mayo*) often invoke *Our Lady of Sorrows* as a symbol of their grief and their resilience in seeking justice for their loved ones.

In Latin American liberation theology, Mary transcends her traditional depictions as passive or silent. Each Marian image—*Our Lady of Guadalupe*, *Aparecida*, and *Sorrows*—symbolizes resistance, hope, and divine solidarity with the oppressed. These depictions inspire transformative action and deepen the theological understanding of God's presence among the marginalized.

RECLAIMING MARY FOR BLACK THEOLOGY

To fully incorporate Mary into Black Theology, there must be:

- **An Afrocentric Reimagining of Mary**: Depicting Mary as a woman of color connected to the struggles of Black women and communities.

- **Contextualized Marian Devotion**: Creating theological and liturgical practices that integrate Mary into the spiritual lives of African Americans, emphasizing her role as a mother, advocate, and liberator.

- **Intersectional Theology**: Drawing on Womanist and Feminist insights to highlight Mary's agency and resistance to oppressive systems.

While researching for resources to support my often-wild theological musings, [Alvin] my attention was drawn to a book on our bookshelf by an emerging/arriving Womanist scholar, Dr. Yolanda Pierce. In her remarkable work, *In My Grandmother's House: Black Women, Faith, and the Stories We Inherit*, Dr. Pierce responds to Black theology's high Christology with a high Mariology. As a scholar rooted in Womanist theology and African American religious traditions, Pierce's approach to Mariology is not simply about elevating Mary in doctrinal terms but rather about reclaiming her as a symbol of resistance, empowerment, and maternal care in the face of oppression. She emphatically stated:

> I have a high Mariology. I love the story of Mary. I think about the many ways in which Black people, Black men and women, are raising children under institutional violence but are still trying to build within them a love of God, a love of church, a love for tradition and culture. The story of Mary resonates for me – the story of how this mother witnesses her child killed. It was state-sanctioned violence. He was martyred. He was lynched. That crucifixion tree is a lynching tree. —Yolanda Pierce (*Sight Magazine*, 2021)

Some Implications of a High Mariology in Black Theology

From the above reflections and examples, a few easy-to-reach ideas emerge toward the developing of high Mariology in Black Theology.

1. **Mary as Theotokos (Mother of God):** Unlike traditional Black Theology, a high Mariology would embrace the title of Mary as Theotokos. The title, Theotokos, recognizes her unique role in the Incarnation. This is not just a doctrinal affirmation but a lens through which to view Mary as a collaborator in God's salvific work. By bearing the Word made flesh, Mary becomes an active participant in the divine plan, embodying agency and divine-human partnership.

2. **Mary as a Symbol of Liberation:** Drawing from Mary's *Magnificat* (Luke 1:46-55) as a proclamation of social justice. Mary is viewed as a prophetic figure who articulates a vision of God's justice that uplifts the lowly and challenges oppressive systems. This liberatory aspect of Mary aligns with the struggles for justice within African American communities, offering a theological framework for resistance and hope.

3. **Mary as a Maternal Archetype:** A high Mariology would reclaim Mary's maternal role as a source of strength, nurturing, and resilience. Mary's motherhood is not idealized in passive terms, such as Western theology and Black churchdom, but understood as active care in the midst of struggle, making her a model for Black women whose mothering often occurs under systemic oppression. A high Mariology emphasizes Mary's strength and steadfastness, particularly at the foot of the cross, where her presence affirms the dignity of grief and solidarity in suffering.

4. **Womanist Perspective:** A high Mariology situates Mary within a Womanist theological framework, which centers on the experiences of Black women and their survival, resistance, and thriving. Mary becomes a symbol of intersectional strength, embodying the dual realities of divine favor and social marginalization as a young, poor, unwed mother in a patriarchal society. A high Mariology invites a reclaiming of Mary as a figure who resonates deeply with the lived realities of Black women.

5. **Mary as a Model for Faithful Engagement with God:** Mary's *fiat*—her acceptance of God's call—demonstrates a model of faithful agency. A high Mariology interprets this moment not as submission but as an empowered choice to partner with God in the work of redemption. This understanding reframes obedience as a liberatory act, especially for those living under systems of oppression.

6. **Reclaiming Mary for African American Christianity:** While Mary has often been underemphasized in Protestant traditions, a high Mariology challenges the Black Church to embrace Mary as a central figure in its theological and spiritual life. It sees Mary as a bridge between African American spirituality and broader Christian traditions, offering a rich repository of symbolism, narrative, and inspiration. We further suggest embracing what we know about blackness and connect with what we're learning about Mary and construct a Black Mariology from the foundation of:

- Mary as **Blackened** (enslaved, oppressed, resilient).

- Mary as **voice** (breaking silence in a silencing church).

- Mary as **mother** (embodying Black maternal agency).

- Mary as **theologian/poet** (Magnificat as liberation song).

- Mary as **co-sufferer and liberator** (in solidarity with crucified peoples).

We offer these few steps to help us reclaim Mary as a vital figure for liberation within African American theology, while bridging gaps between traditional and contemporary struggles for justice. We are confident that emerging theologians can adequately resolve the tension between the construct of Mary past to an empowered vision of a liberating Mary.

A post from April 2012, written by a graduate student, summed up the historical polarity this way: "Roman Catholic Mariology draws people away from Jesus and towards Mary," whereas Protestantism draws people away from Mary toward Jesus.

DISCUSSION QUESTIONS

1. How has Mary been presented in your church community?

2. Are you familiar with the concept of Mariology? If so, how so?

3. What are your thoughts on Catholicism's presentation of Mary as the Mother of God (Theotokos)?

4. Which of the Latin memorials of Mary appeals to you?

5. If your church erected a memorial of Mary, what would it represent?

6. What are your thoughts on shaping a High Mariology in Black or Womanist theology? What would you add to it beyond what the author has suggested?

Chapter 4

THE SEVEN SAYINGS OF MARY AS PREACHED AT BETHLEHEM MISSIONARY BAPTIST CHURCH, RICHMOND, CALIFORNIA ADVENT 2023

"Though Mary has often been cast as a silent figure, Scripture records her words in moments that demand our attention. These sayings, small in number but vast in depth, offer a liberatory framework that has yet to be fully embraced. What might happen if we listened to Mary again?"

Mary as a Model for Transformative Dialogue

We did not go looking for Mary. Mary found us and challenged us to reconsider the Black church's relationship to her. As a result, my beloved wife and I propose that Mary's recorded sayings offer a framework for engaging in liberatory dialogue—conversations that empower the marginalized, disrupt oppressive systems, and envision a world aligned with God's justice. We use her voice as a pivotal moment in the Gospel narrative, demonstrating the transformative potential of speaking truth in the face of power.

For us both, preaching is an act of breaking the silence. Black preachers preaching about Black life, rather than repeating white theological lies, break the silence. When women stand to preach, their standing alone breaks the silence. God forbid they have something to say! We are both students and practitioners of the dialectical model of preaching, particularly as taught and wonderfully modelled by the late Dr. Samuel Dewitt Proctor. I provide a workbook that reframes *Dr. Proctor's dialectical approach in Preaching Sermons that Matter: A Workbook on the Dialectical Model as Taught by Samuel Dewitt Proctor* (Bernstine, 2023).

For forty years, I served as Lead Pastor in Black Baptist churches in the South and the East Coast. I ended my pastoral journey on the so-called liberal West Coast. Ironically, I found the resistance to women in ministry and the continued silencing of women's voices more obstinate on the West Coast than in the so-called conservative South. In Black church life, the minimization of Mary's voice mirrors broader social dynamics, where the voices of marginalized groups, particularly Black women, are often silenced or overlooked. While the Black Church has historically been a space of empowerment, it has also, at times, mirrored patriarchal norms that restrict women's roles and voices. This tension creates a missed opportunity to elevate Mary's words as a source of theological depth and social transformation.

By contrast, Mary's sayings provide a counter-narrative to this silencing. Her *Magnificat* calls for a world where the lowly are elevated, her *fiat* (her consent at the Annunciation) exemplifies the power of a personal "yes" to God's call, and her silent yet steadfast presence at the crucifixion models a resilience that speaks volumes. We've retained in the written text most of our preaching voices and cadences. Being manuscript preachers made the translation that much easier.

Prefacing each sermon are artistic renderings from a phenomenal African American woman artist, Yvonne Simmons of Third New Hope Baptist Church, Detroit, Michigan. We also offer a thought on the theological categories and homiletical frames behind each sermonic idea. We pray Mary finds you in the following preaching experiences.

DISCUSSION QUESTIONS

1. How has Mary been preached in your church tradition?

2. What has been the position on women's voices in your church?

THE FIRST SAYING OF MARY: POWER FOR DIVINE CONFUSION

First Sunday of Advent, 2023

Reverend Dr. Alvin C. Bernstine

The Theological Category: *Mariology of Disruption*

The Homiletical Frame: Mary's confusion before Gabriel becomes a theological lens for divine interruption. God's favor unsettles human control and creates space for new beginnings.

TEXT: *In the sixth month, the angel Gabriel was sent by God to a town in Galilee called*

Nazareth,²⁷ to a virgin engaged to a man whose name was Joseph, of the house of David. The virgin's name was Mary. ²⁸ And he came to her and said, "Greetings, favored one! The Lord is with you."²⁹ But she was much perplexed by his words and pondered what sort of greeting this might be. ³⁰ The angel said to her, "Do not be afraid, Mary, for you have found favor with God.³¹ And now, you will conceive in your womb and bear a son, and you will name him Jesus.³² He will be great, and will be called the Son of the Most High, and the Lord God will give to him the throne of his ancestor David.³³ He will reign over the house of Jacob forever, and of his kingdom there will be no end."³⁴ Mary said to the angel, "How can this be, since I am a virgin?"³⁵ The angel said to her, "The Holy Spirit will come upon you, and the power of the Most High will overshadow you; therefore, the child to be born will be holy; he will be called Son of God.³⁶ And now, your relative Elizabeth in her old age has also conceived a son; and this is the sixth month for her who was said to be barren.³⁷ For nothing will be impossible with God." —(Luke 1:27-37, NRSV)

In my meditative reading, I ran across a powerful observation about great stories. Scott Erikson (2020), in his marvelous little book, *Honest Advent*, states, **"All great stories come at a cost."** Mary is part of a great story. In fact, Mary's story is great. Her story is so great that it is in the Bible. Her story is so great that images of Mary are seen all over the world. Her story is so great that many of us include her in our Christmas programs, poems, and decorations every year. Every Sunday in many churches, her name is mentioned in a faith statement known as the Apostle's Creed:

> **I believe in God, the Father Almighty, Creator of Heaven and earth; and in Jesus Christ, His only Son, Our Lord, Who was conceived by the Holy Ghost, born of the Virgin Mary, suffered under Pontius Pilate, was crucified, died, and was buried.**

Mary's story is great because one day, an angel showed up and announced favor in her life. **"Greetings, favored one! The Lord is with you."** In the thinking of our culture and church, most of us here would welcome an announcement that God has found favor in us. In fact, from what I hear, God has found favor in some folks. Testimonies abound declaring, **"I'm blessed and highly favored!"** However, when we read our text, the angelic announcement of Mary being favored does not evoke an "I'm-blessed-and-highly-favored" testimony. The announcement confused her. The text says, **"But she was much perplexed by his words and pondered what sort of greeting this might be."** Her response was not, "Hallelujah! Praise the Lord! Or I'm blessed and highly favored." Her response was to be perplexed, bewildered, and troubled. She was confused, for one, by the visit, and more confused over the announcement.

I know the Bible says, **"God is not the author of confusion."** But I looked at the word, and the word for confusion used by Paul in 1 Corinthians 14:33 is not the same word used in our text, nor in the same context. The word used by Luke implies that Mary was deeply agitated and emotionally disturbed. She was greatly alarmed. She was troubled, anxious, and uncertain about being a recipient of a message of being favored by God. For all practical purposes, Mary was confused. The dominant emotion described in this story is confusion. Once the angel laid out the plan of what being favored involved, Mary's response expressed confusion. She said, *"How can this be, since I am a virgin?"*

I want to propose today that **Mary's first word invites us to consider the life-altering possibilities of responding to the moments when what God wants from us confuses us**. I hope to impress upon someone, hopefully, the Bethlehem Church Family, that announcements of God's favor are experiences of divine confusion, and we need power for divine confusion. Being favored by God never means our lives remain the same. Being favored by God rarely fits our plans or accommodates our story. Mary, being favored by God, didn't fit into her story; this caused her confusion.

God's favor for Mary confused her because it changed her story. It went against everything she believed, including what she believed about herself. It disrupted the plans she had for her life, and it literally changed the script for how she believed faith operated. People of faith must allow for moments when God's plans for our lives are confusing. Our greatest contribution to the drama of faith is to accept that God's way of bringing something new into the world confuses us. Isaiah says, *"God's ways are not our ways. God's thoughts are not our thoughts."*

Mary is presented as a person of faith. She is presented as a member of the faith community and has a connection with God. However, her faith perspective was packaged in a belief system that suggested that if you do this, God will do that. It was a system of belief that gave her some control over her life, even in a context where women were systemically disempowered. Yet, her faith allowed her to work out the details of her life in alignment with subscribed beliefs. Yes, there was God! There was scripture and church, but she believed she had a measure of control over her life, her story, and yes, her body. Yet, she needed something she had never needed before, and that was power for divine confusion.

Like so many of us, Mary's response to God's announcement reveals that anything outside of her belief system was confusing, including an angelic visit with an announcement of God's favor. Mary's confusion speaks to us who hold belief systems that if you do this, God will do that. Her confusion speaks to us who believe in angels, but we ain't trying to see one or hear from one. Like Mary, we want a belief system that provides us with a measure of control over our lives. We want our story to be our story, and we want some measure of control with the script.

We come to church if we feel like it, or stay at home if we want. We give whatever we want to give, or we don't give anything at all. We serve when we want to serve, or we don't serve at all. Mary's confusion speaks to us who have stories and scripts that we want to live out, and it doesn't include any announcement from God that changes our story or disrupts our script. Scott Erikson challenged us more when he added that not only do great stories cost, but when God makes an announcement in our life, our story comes to an end. Whatever we had planned, it's over! Finished! **"The rub of revelation is that it's a transformation you're not in charge of"** (Erikson, 2020, p. 28).

I have some preacher-pastor friends who have serious control issues. They clearly don't know how to deal with divine confusion. They take "overseer" way too literally and much too seriously. They want to oversee everything and everyone. They have not responded well to divine confusion. Here's the problem with it: when God calls us, we know that we are no longer in charge of our own lives, so why are we trying to be in charge of everyone else's life? Our story changes, and when the story changes, we need to find a way to access power for divine confusion. We have to get okay with being like Mary and ask: **How? Why? What? When? or Really?**

At least one person ought to be asking how we accommodate the power for divine confusion. I only have two observations from the text, one of which potentially changes everything we have ever believed about the Mary story. The first observation I want to call **virgin space**. What we have been taught and believe about Mary is that she was a virgin. It's in the text. ***In the sixth month, the angel Gabriel was sent by God to a town in Galilee called Nazareth, to a virgin engaged to a man whose name was Joseph, of the house of David. The virgin's name was Mary."*** It's how she is introduced into the story, and it's even how she understood herself. *"How can this be, since I am a virgin?"*

The concept of Mary the Virgin has been viewed through the sexualization of Western theology. As an issue of sex, we limit the possibilities of the text to the purity of women and the morality of divine selection. Virgin as a sexual reality and a moral standard misinterprets the powerful intent of the text by limiting it to gender and morality. If the only people eligible for God birthing new realities are sexual virgins, most of us will never birth a new reality into the world. We will be stuck in our old stories and old beliefs.

Virgin, from the Jewish Kabbalist perspective, was not limited to sexual purity, nor was it a moral issue. Virgin was not just a physical attribute. It was a spiritual orientation. **Virginity was a theological concept that implied holding a special space for divine influence.** Like a woman preserving herself, virginity suggests holding a special place for divine influence. Although Mary held a belief system that believed that if you do this, God will do that, she also held a sacred space for divine influence. It was not physical; it was spiritual. Mary held a virgin space.

Let me make this plain. Most of us here know we've lived stories where we wanted to control the story. In our stories, we were at the center, and on the throne, if you please. God couldn't do anything through us, because God couldn't do anything with us. Yet, the reason why you are here today is that despite all your self-centered insanity, you hold a sacred space that's open for divine influence. The wise among us know that we are not at the center. We've learned that we don't do well on the throne, and God has empowered us to become different, a new birth, if you please, because we possessed a virgin space. Even now, some of us can "act a fool" all week, but we make our way to the Lord's house because we have preserved a sacred space for divine influence. Our virgin space allows God to birth something new in us in order to give us a new story. Some of us can testify that the old story was going to kill us, but the new story gives us life. The old story was taking us nowhere, but the new story helps us to see that the best is yet to come.

Maybe that's not clear enough. Can I testify? I'm here today, not because I've been so good or acted so holy. I'm here because, as sinful as I have been, and as crazy as I've behaved, I've always held a sacred space for divine influence. I was blessed with a praying grandmother, grandfather, mother, and father, who saw something in me that I didn't see in myself. Like the prodigal son, I've been in the far country. I've lived among swine, but even among the swine, I preserved a sacred space where God could birth something new in my life and make me into something I could have never made myself.

The reason why the Lord calls us to love everybody is because the Lord knows that even the most hateful person possesses a sacred/virgin space that can be impregnated with divine influence. Bethle-hem, the reason we keep these doors open is to give an opportunity for God to birth something new in virgin space. The angel might show up in a song. The angel might speak through a testimony, an encouraging word, a hug, and sometimes, a sermon. However and whenever the angel shows up, it's because God recognizes virgin spaces.

Yet even with that, Mary asks, *"How can this be, since I am a virgin?"* This leads me to the final observation. I want to label this **Spirit space**. The angel said, *"The Holy Spirit will come upon you, and the power of the Most High will overshadow you ...."* Mary had a belief system. She believed in God. She had a story and a plan for her life. She also had a virgin story, where she held a sacred place for divine influence. Mary had virgin space, but virgin space alone doesn't birth a new reality. Virgin space alone can be confusing because of human limitations. Her confusion, however, was, *"How can this be?"*

Power for divine confusion is that God doesn't leave us to work things out for ourselves, or by ourselves. God knows we are limited creatures, but Mary's first word positions us to see that divine in-fluence includes divine power. Virgin space opens up the opportunity for Spirit space. The Holy Spirit will do in us what God wants done. And when the Holy Spirit shows up, we discern *"For nothing will be impossible with God."*

Someone needs to hear me, today. The Spirit of God overcomes confusion. God's Spirit overcomes doubts and limitations. God's Spirit will even overcome our limited belief systems and do something in us that only God can do. *"For nothing will be impossible with God."* We may not see how the story is going to work out, but with God, nothing is impossible. We may not see where the story is going. Truthfully, I don't know how my story is going to work out. I don't even know where my story is going, but after 47 years of trying to preach the gospel, sometimes up and sometimes down, I can testify, *"For nothing will be impossible with God."*

Bethlehem, don't limit God to our capabilities. Don't try to control what God wants to work out. God knows about the level of our confusion, but God still wants to birth a new reality in our church. God provides power for divine confusion, and it will take people with virgin spaces and receptive spirits for God's Spirit. ***"For nothing will be impossible with God."***

DISCUSSION QUESTIONS

1. How have you interpreted the angel's visitation to Mary?

2. Do you have any experiences with God that confused you? If so, how did you respond?

3. Has God done anything great in your life? What did it cost?

4. Do you have a place in your life reserved for divine influence? What do you call it?

5. Who are the people God used to guide you out of confusion?

Chapter 6

THE SECOND SAYING OF MARY: FROM CONFUSION TO SUBMISSION

Second Sunday of Advent, 2023
Reverend Dr. Alvin C. Bernstine

The Theological Category: *Mariology of Surrender*

The Homiletical Frame: Mary's "Yes" is a theology of courageous submission, not passivity. It is the radical defiance of oppressive norms by choosing alignment with God's liberating will.

TEXT: *"I am the Lord's servant. May it be to me as you have said."* (Luke 1:38)

I love a great story, and as Scott Erikson noted, **"All great stories come at a cost."** Imagine the story of a woman named Keisha who grew up in a historically marginalized neighborhood, where opportunities were scarce, and poverty was a constant and ugly presence. From a young age, Keisha had a passion for education and a dream to become a teacher. However, the odds seemed stacked against her—underfunded schools, systemic inequality, and limited access to quality education.

One day, while walking through the community, something lit a fire in her. Keisha witnessed a group of children struggling to read, their crusty eyes filled with frustration and defeat. The neighborhood had a long history of educational disparities, and Keisha couldn't stand to see another generation left behind. It was then that she felt a calling, a deep conviction that she should become a teacher and be a source of inspiration and empowerment for her community.

Despite the financial challenges and the doubts of some who questioned her dream, Keisha chose to surrender to God's calling. She worked tirelessly to earn her degree, working multiple jobs to support herself through school. She trusted in God's plan, believing that if she remained obedient to her calling, she could make a difference.

Years later, Keisha not only became a teacher but also founded an after-school program in her home church, providing tutoring and mentorship to countless children. She became a symbol of hope and resilience, demonstrating what can be achieved when one surrenders to God's will, even in the face of stiff adversity. I've dropped into the text and the second saying of Mary, just as Keisha's obedience led to transformation and empowerment in her neighborhood, Mary's submission to God's will in Luke 1:38 played a pivotal role in bringing hope and liberation to a marginalized community, and a Savior into the world.

The second saying of Mary invites us into the new thing God wants to do by moving us from confusion to submission. Thus, I propose that **to live into the new reality that God wants to bring into the world, we must move from confusion into submission.** The shift from confusion into submission represents the pivotal moment when we defy any and every life restraint and decide to participate in the liberating possibilities of God. Submission is a conscious act to surrender to a higher power or greater cause. Submission happens when we decide to no longer be defined by cultural and social limitations and expectations, but by our willingness to be defined by God's new reality.

Mary essentially announces, **"What I've been, I will be no longer. Whatever cultural and social norms that have constrained me, they no longer have power over me. While I may have been confused about my capacity to participate in God's reality, I'm going to submit to God's capacity to do with me what I could never do with myself, or by myself."** *"I am the Lord's servant. May it be as you have said."*

We ought to be rallied by Mary's words. Her words ought to serve as marching orders for all of us whose lives have been limited by cultural, social, and economic expectations. Cultural, social, and economic expectations limit new-life possibilities, especially when those expectations are shaded by ominous and ubiquitous oppression. Too much of who we are and what we do is limited by the life-suffocating realities of race, gender, and economically based oppression. As people of faith, we ought to be lining up behind Mary's words because religion, too often, reinforces the limitations of cultural and social expectations. The American church, inclusive of the Black church, has allowed itself to be evangelized by the culture rather than evangelizing the culture. We no longer turn the world upside down but allow the world to turn us upside down and inside out. The views of the world too often become the views of the church, rather than the views of the church becoming the views of the world.

Yes, this can be confusing when faith preaches "all things are possible" and the church lives in limitations. It's confusing to claim to serve a good God but be surrounded by so many bad things. It's confusing to claim God as a God of love and be surrounded by so much hate. It's confusing to claim to serve a God with all power, and we exercise no power.

Mary's word of submission is a radical shift that positions her to defy both Roman oppression and Jewish patriarchy. She was a child raised in a world defined by an oppressive power and lived under the roof of a people who not only conceded to Roman oppression but perpetuated their own systems of oppression. Just as hurt people hurt people, oppressed people oppress people. Colonized people colonize people. If oppression is pain and limitations, Mary's world was defined by pain and limitations. The pain of Roman oppression and the limitations of Jewish patriarchy. Her world was a confusing mess of pervasive needs and unchecked greed.

Some of us grew up identifying oppression as **"the man."** **"The man"** personified the evil power that we experienced as being under siege by the oppression of white supremacy. **"The man"** was in control, even control of our bodies. **"The man"** was the nebulous, but definitive personality of the forces that threatened us with violence if we dared defy our social limitations. If we did anything other than what we were doing, we were warned of the consequences of being on the wrong side of **"the man."** If we tried to be anything other than what we were, we did so at the risk of the wrath of **"the man."** If we were going to go anywhere beyond our context of pain and limitation, we would need the permission of **"the man."**

Perhaps one of the contributors to the rising levels of mental illness in our communities is the confusion precipitated by oppressed people oppressing people. Think about it! It literally can drive people crazy when their whole world is defined by pain and limitations. It gets crazier when the dominant response to pain and limitations is the embrace of a religion of a God no one sees, and only a few people hear from. Mary had to be confused when an angel of the Lord showed up in her space of pain and limitations, spoke to her, a poor teenage girl of an oppressed people, and declared God's favor.

Of greater interest in the text is that God's intervention in the world demonstrated God getting involved where life begins for all of us—motherhood! Life begins for all of us in the amazing miracle of motherhood. If the Bible tells us anything from Eve to Mary, God's new thing begins with motherhood. Dr. Jacqueline Thompson, pastor of Allen Temple, observed that whenever God wants to do something new, he uses a woman. From a barren Sarah and Hannah, a rejected Leah and Hagar, to Elizabeth and Mary, God used the miracle of motherhood as the vessel for God's new thing.

Think about it! Who suffers most in a world of pain and limitations? Mothers! Who feels the most pain of bearing children who have no future? Mothers! Who is most traumatized when an oppressive power violently responds to an oppressed people's angry desperation with 60-plus days of non-stop bombs and bullets, bombs and bullets, wreaking injury and death, injury and death?[14] Mothers! God used the miracle of motherhood in the shift from confusion to submission.

Mary shifts from the induced confusion of a world of pain and limitations and submits to God's new thing. I don't know about you, but I want to join Mary and move from a space of confusion and be a willing participant in the new thing God wants done. As I read this text through the lens of Mary's world of pain and limitations, a couple of things show up as opportunities for us to participate in God's new thing. I see an opportunity for the move when we submit to a **sense of a new identity** and a **new sense of the power of God's Word** as essential to participating in God's new thing.

I need you to come closer to the text and view the shift from the confusion of a poor, teenage girl of a marginalized community, living under the siege of "the man," and the oppression of male patriarchy. There is a noted shift in her understanding of who she was when she declares, *"I am the Lord's servant."* She walked out of a world that defined her as an object to accommodate a male culture and as a subject of an oppressive power, and claimed a new sense of identity.

We, too, walk out of confusion once we submit to the transforming power of God that gifts us with an identity consistent with our possibilities and assignment. Mary says, *"I am the Lord's servant."* "I'm no longer limited by age, by gender, by poverty, by marginalization, or oppression." Like Jesus's seven "I am" statements, where he embraced an identity consistent with his assignment. She says, "**I am the Lord's servant, not Caesar's subject, not Joseph's wife, not a slave, not a poor girl, not a powerless, oppressed, marginalized person.**"

You walk out of confusion when there is **a new sense of you consistent with your possibilities and assignment.** It doesn't matter what the people call you or how the world sees you; submission to God's assignment comes with a new identity. Like Kunta Kinte in Roots. You can call me Toby, a person experiencing pain and limitations, but I know who I am: *"I am the Lord's servant."* Like Celie in The Color Purple, you can call me stupid, ugly, everything but a child of God, but I know who I am: *"I am the Lord's servant."* You can label me a slave, someone's property, or a tool of "the man," but

---

14 Israel's response to the October 7, 2023 assault of the Palestinians on concert attending Israelites and unarmed Kibbutz dwellers. Israel used superior weaponry to brutally kill and destroy Palestinians, mostly innocent women and children.

like Nat Turner or Sojourner Truth, I know who I am: *"I am the Lord's servant."* You can minimize me and try to dehumanize me, but I know who I am: *"I am the Lord's servant."* Whenever we submit to God's assignment, it demands an identity consistent with our possibilities and the assignment set before us. *"I am the Lord's servant."* It's a refusal to be defined by the confusing definitions of the culture and society. *"I am the Lord's servant."* I have an identity consistent with my assignment, and I'm walking out of confusion into submission.

The second thing that leaps from the text is Mary's submission to **a new sense of the power of God's Word.** She submitted to a capacity consistent with her possibilities and assignment. She also submitted to God's Word as a power she could live with. In a space of confusion, she walked into submission. *"May it be to me as you have said."* Please don't run past Gabriel too quickly. Gabriel was more than a winged white person showing up in Black space. Gabriel represented an authentic expression of God's involvement in the affairs of human beings. An angel signals that God is getting involved! Look at it closer! God's intent to intervene in the world was being communicated to a poor, teenage girl of a marginalized people who was suffering at the hands of an oppressive power. Whatever was going on in Mary's world, God not only wanted to do something about it, but God wanted Mary to be a part of what God was up to. An angel, a messenger of God, spoke a word of God to a person of God about the conditions of the people of God, and God's intent to do something about it. She heard God's word like never before. She submitted to a power consistent with her God-given possibilities and assignment.

A new sense of the power of God's Word is its ability to break through the limitations of culture and society and birth something new into the world. God's Word becomes not something filtered through the religious machinery of culture and society, but a word of power that speaks clearly about God's intentions in the world. Scott Erikson helps us again when he makes the distinction between the mechanics of faith versus the essence of faith (Erickson, 2020). The mechanics of faith are our need to make visible what is invisible. The essence is the invisible manifestation of God's presence and/or power. The essence of God's Word is a manifestation of power; the mechanics of God's Word take the form of a leather-bound book, written in a language we understand, or a Bible app on a phone or computer.

Church and Christmas have become so mechanical that we miss the essence of both. The mechanics of the church are buildings, budgets, business, pews, programs, and technologies. Yet, the essence of the church is the Holy Spirit acting in power among God's people. The essence of God's Word is a fugitive from justice showing up at Pharaoh's house, knocking on the door, and demanding, *"Let my people go!"* The essence of God's Word is a once enslaved brother standing at the Jordan submitting to God's Word, *"Be strong and of good courage. Do not be afraid, nor dismayed, for the Lord your God is with you wherever you go."*

The mechanics of Christmas are December 25, Christmas trees, lights, presents, Santa Claus, and reindeer. However, the essence of Christmas is God doing a new thing in the world to demonstrate God's love. We too often miss the essence of God wanting to do something new in the world. God has extended an invitation to us to join God in God's work. The mechanics of God's word are a leather-bound book, an app, or a computer screen. The essence of God's Word is a woman submitting to the power of God's Word, showing up in the Temple, and the pastor confusing fervent prayer with a woman being drunk.

The essence of God's Word is Esther submitting to the power of God's word, daring to go before the King and declaring, **"If I perish, I perish."** The essence of God's Word is a jailed preacher submitting to the power of God's Word and proclaiming to a colonized church, **"I can do all things through Christ who strengthens me."** The essence of God's Word is a Black preacher of the Jim Crow South submitting to the power of God's Word, demanding that America, **"Let justice run down like water and righteousness like a mighty stream."** The essence of God's Word is a girl born into a patriarchally painful and limiting Bethlehem Missionary Baptist Church who becomes a woman who submits to the power of God's Word and is positioned to become its first woman pastor because *"God will pour out his Spirit on all flesh, and God's sons and daughters shall prophecy."* The move from confusion to submission is to submit to God's power to give us an identity and the capacity to fit the assignment of God's new thing. **HALLELUJAH! PRAISE GOD'S NAME!**

DISCUSSION QUESTIONS

1. What comes up for you when you hear the word "submission"? Is it a positive thought or a negative one?

2. Mary's world was defined by the limitations of Roman oppression and patriarchy. What defines the limitations of your world?

3. How does the way you see yourself connect with your assignment and possibilities?

4. Are you able to make the distinctions between the "mechanics" of faith and the "essence" of faith? Give some examples.

5. Share a moment in your life where God's word brought you out of confusion?

Chapter 7

Bethlehem Missionary Baptist Church
The Advent Series – The Third Saying of Mary

Luke 1:39-45
THE THIRD SAYING OF MARY: SISTER TO SISTER

Third Sunday of Advent, 2023
Reverend Diana Becton

The Theological Category: *Mariology of Solidarity*

The Homiletical Frame: Mary's greeting to Elizabeth creates safe space, holy vulnerability, and Spirit-filled affirmation. This is a theology of mutual recognition among marginalized women.

Sermonic Prayer: Almighty God, grant us the grace to hope in you with unwavering trust. As we begin this season of Advent, may our hearts be filled with the hope that comes from knowing your promises are true and that you are still doing new things. Amen.

"In those days, Mary set out and went with haste to a Judean town in the hill country, [40] where she entered the house of Zechariah and greeted Elizabeth. [41] When Elizabeth heard Mary's greeting, the child leaped in her womb. And Elizabeth was filled with the Holy Spirit [42] and exclaimed with a loud cry, "Blessed are you among women, and blessed is the fruit of your womb. [43] And why has this happened to me, that the mother of my Lord comes to me? [44] For as soon as I heard your greeting, the child in my womb leaped for joy. [45] And blessed is she who believed that there would be a fulfillment of what was spoken to her by the Lord." (Luke 1:39-45 NRSV)

Title: Sister-to-Sister (The title is borrowed from Sister Renita Weems's Award Winning Publication)

Since the beginning of civilization, there have been encounters in one form or another that changed the course of nations, changed the destiny of individuals, and changed the world. Think of the day when Moses met God at the burning bush or when David faced Goliath on the battlefield. Recall the moment when the apostle Paul encountered the risen Christ on the road to Damascus, transforming him from a persecutor to a preacher of the Gospel. These are all great encounters that changed the world.

Think about encounters between Black intellectual pioneers like Booker T. Washington and W.E.B. DuBois, who paved the way for the Civil Rights Movement. Booker T. Washington was born into slavery, his father an unknown white man, and his mother an enslaved Black woman who was eventually emancipated. W.E.B. DuBois was born free, into privilege, educated in white schools, and obtained a PhD from Harvard. Both men wanted the same thing—socioeconomic equality for Blacks in America—but based on their experiences, they formed two contrasting opinions on how to get there. Their ideas about the road to freedom differed, and Blacks did not completely agree with either side; however, their encounters and the intersection of their ideas changed lives and got people to thinking about the best way for Black people to achieve equality in a racist world when 40 acres and a mule seemed like a good deal.

Today, our attention turns to an encounter between two women, Mary, the mother-to-be of Jesus, and Elizabeth, the mother-to-be of John the Baptist, whose encounter was marked by an unusual greeting. It was a greeting that literally represented a *confirmation of the new thing God was ushering into the world through the marginalized and exploited.* That is what we are going to talk about because I see in these two women a greeting that clearly represents a new thing that God was doing. Both women are positioned to be used by God to birth into the world two of the most pivotal people in the history of our faith community.

Perhaps it may be helpful for us to explore some of the meanings of greetings. Greetings establish a framework for interaction, indicating the beginning of a social exchange and setting the tone for subsequent communication. At a fundamental level, greetings serve as a form of acknowledgment and recognition, signaling respect, politeness, belonging, acceptance, and inclusion. A greeting basically says, "I see you." Any of us who were either born in the South or had Southern parents know that when you encounter someone you know, you don't just walk by without saying something. Oh no! You slow down, pause, and offer a greeting. You acknowledge and recognize the other person, especially if they are older than you. What was being impressed upon us was our responsibility to affirm one another, to establish a connection, and to show respect for one another.

We have lost so much of this way of greeting one another. Perhaps this explains some of the rude disconnectedness we are experiencing in our community today. No one is greeting or acknowledging one another's existence or humanity. People walk into a home and don't speak. Folks live in the same home and don't even greet each other when they start the day. We even show up at church in the Lord's house and don't say a word to one another. Sometimes, we just rush by folks, too preoccupied with our own stuff, our own business, to even acknowledge one another. And when we do speak, it is perfunctory or trivialized by formality. Am I right about it?

However, the greeting between Mary and Elizabeth was different! There was something different that drove the greeting between the two women. Although the actual words of the greeting are not stated in the text, a sister-to-sister connection was made, unlike the greetings shaped by the power dynamics of the culture, where women spoke to men differently than they spoke to women, and how people without power spoke to people with power, or the courteous exchanges between the rich and the poor. It was not a greeting colored with the empty niceties of race. The greeting was a sister-to-sister exchange. Both Mary and Elizabeth were bearing unusual burdens, and they both needed more than just a formal salutation. Their exchange was more than a greeting; it had to do with how they saw one another, and that is as beloved sisters in a common struggle. It was a sister-to-sister greeting because a sister-to-sister greeting shares the moment, embraces the common struggles, and somehow finds joy in the midst of the struggle. A sister-to-sister greeting offers a word that communicates deep feelings, respect, and affection.

Perhaps we might want to consider how different our greetings would be if they had the potential to bring something new into the world. If our biblical sisters could help us, they would inform us that in this sister-to-sister greeting, Mary entered the house of Zechariah and greeted Elizabeth. The first thing we note is that the greeting between Mary and Elizabeth **opened opportunities for shaping safe spaces.**

We need safe spaces because safe spaces provide a place of support for those who have shared experiences. This is critical for those of us who have been marginalized, exploited, harassed, and criticized. In the text, Mary hastened to see Elizabeth, and there she found a sister who offered a safe space that conveyed, "I believe you. I see you. I'm here for you. Come, here is a place of refuge, to find comfort, and to be nurtured." Elizabeth opened her home, her arms, and her heart.

Here at BMBC, whenever we create a new small group, whether it is a Bible study class or Tuesday talks, we share something called "core values." We talk about things like the importance of confidentiality. What is said in the group stays in the group. We commit to all doing our part to create an environment where everyone can be real, open, and honest in their struggles and victories. We agree to value one another during the discussions by really listening to what is being shared. What we are really doing is being intentional about creating safe spaces where everyone can be valued and accepted.

Safe spaces provide a platform for us to feel seen, to share our stories, and to offer a place to belong. Putting it simply, safe spaces are those places where people feel they can just be who they are. They give us an opportunity to feel valued, included, and connected. To be in a safe space provides an invitation to be affirmed as a part of the community and as children of God. We need safe spaces. Secondly, when the safe space was opened, the Bible says, ***"When Elizabeth heard the greeting of Mary, the baby leaped in her womb."*** What Elizabeth had shamefully hidden for six months showed up and showed out. The greeting between Mary and Elizabeth, even in Zechariah's house, **opened the opportunity for holy vulnerability.**

We need **opportunities to be vulnerable!**

What would it mean to you, my sister, and even to you, my brother, if you could truly be vulnerable about the new thing God is working in your life? I understand that it won't be easy. Like Elizabeth, there may be things happening in your life right now that are causing you anxiety and shame, but a life-affirming connection with another sister can trigger a kick from the new thing God wants to bring into the world. That's the work that we have been doing in Christian Empowerment Hour (Bethlehem's version of church school). Reading books like Kellye Fabian's *Holy Vulnerability* (Fabian, 2021), we recognize that we all carry places of anxiety, shame, and fear, and struggle with accepting that we are broken. But at the same time, we acknowledge that it's okay.

Ashamed of things you have done? It's okay!

Recovering from addiction? It's okay!

Have you been domineering and controlling? It's okay!

Because right here, you can find and reach out to a sister or brother and make a life-affirming connection that lets you know it is okay. And just like what happened to Elizabeth when the baby kicked in her womb, you, too, can make a life-affirming connection that triggers the kick you need to joyfully bring forth the new thing that God wants to bring into the world through you. May we, like Elizabeth and Mary, trust that God has taken away our shame and become a community that supports each other. Sharing our vulnerable places allows room to trigger the new thing God wants to bring into the world. We need opportunities to be vulnerable.

Finally, the sister-to-sister greeting between Mary and Elizabeth **opened the opportunity for the manifestation of the Holy Spirit.** The sister-to-sister connection allowed the Holy Spirit to give Elizabeth something that both she and Mary needed. Elizabeth acknowledged and celebrated the new thing God was working out in Mary's life. The Bible says, "Elizabeth was filled with the Holy Spirit and exclaimed with a loud cry, 'Blessed are you among women, and blessed is the fruit of your womb'" (Luke 1:41-42). She finally had an opportunity to embrace and celebrate what God was doing in her life, saying, "And why has this happened to me, that the mother of my Lord comes to me? For as soon as I heard your greeting, the child in my womb leaped for joy. And blessed is she who believed that there would be a fulfillment of what was spoken to her by the Lord"(Luke 1:43-45).

Essentially, Elizabeth is celebrating how God has shown up and done some new things. She is celebrating God's divine interventions in both of their lives. This reminds us that God specializes in turning the impossible into the possible. In our own lives, we can find hope in knowing that God is still doing new things. Do you need a kickstart in your life? Through God, all things are possible. Nothing is impossible for God.

DISCUSSION QUESTIONS

1. Name some encounters that impacted the way you see life.

2. What does having safe spaces mean to you?

3. Who are the people in your life who make you feel safe?

4. What does vulnerability mean to you?

5. Who in your life celebrates your experiences with God?

Chapter 8

THE FOURTH SAYING OF MARY: GROWN FOLKS' MUSIC:
When Christmas Grows Up

Fourth Sunday in Advent 2023
Reverends Alvin C. Bernstine and Diana Becton

The Theological Category: *Mariology of Liberation Song*

The Homiletical Frame: The Magnificat as freedom music—grown folk's lyrics that center justice, mercy, and divine reversal. Mary sings theology into existence as protest and praise.

ALVIN - TEXT: [46]*And Mary said, "My soul magnifies the Lord, [47]and my spirit rejoices in God my Savior, [48]for he has looked with favor on the lowliness of his servant. Surely, from now on all generations will call me blessed; [49]for the Mighty One has done great things for me, and holy is his name. [50]His mercy is for those who fear him from generation to generation. [51]He has shown strength with his arm; he has scattered the proud in the thoughts of their hearts. [52]He has brought down the powerful from their thrones, and lift-*

ed up the lowly; ⁵³he has filled the hungry with good things, and sent the rich away empty. ⁵⁴He has helped his servant Israel, in remembrance of his mercy, ⁵⁵according to the promise he made to our ancestors, to Abraham and to his descendants forever." ⁵⁶And Mary remained with her about three months and then returned to her home." (Luke 1:46-56, NRSV)

DIANA - *And Mary said, I'm bursting with God-news; I'm dancing the song of my Savior God. God took one good look at me, and look what happened—I'm the most fortunate woman on earth! What God has done for me will never be forgotten, the God whose very name is holy, set apart from all others. His mercy flows in wave after wave on those who are in awe before him. He bared his arm and showed his strength, scattered the bluffing braggarts. He knocked tyrants off their high horses, pulled victims out of the mud. The starving poor sat down to a banquet; the callous rich were left out in the cold. He embraced his chosen child, Israel; he remembered and piled on the mercies, piled them high. It's exactly what he promised, beginning with Abraham and right up to now." (Luke 1:46-46, The Message)*

ALVIN: Imagine a Christmas that musically invites us beyond the manger scene into the heart of a revolutionary song. We both love music, so this should be exciting. It started last week with your message, *Sister to Sister*. An older woman and a younger woman, both carrying unexpected babies, connecting in grown folks' space, facing grown folks' realities, having grown folks' talk. Both women internalize their now unexpected realities and put to song what was alive in their spirit. They sang grown folks' music.

As soon as Mary walked through the door and spoke, Elizabeth's baby leaped, and she began to sing. Mary greeted, but the sound of Mary's greeting moved Elizabeth to sing. She sang, "**Blessed are you among women, and blessed is the child you will bear! But why am I so favored that the mother of my Lord should come to me? As soon as the sound of your greeting reached my ears, the baby in my womb leaped for joy. Blessed is she who has believed that the Lord would fulfill his promises to her!**"

DIANA: I see where the scripture helps us to understand why Elizabeth started to sing. The Bible says she became filled with the Holy Spirit, and whatever else we know about the Holy Spirit, the Holy Spirit will make you sing. You might not be known to sing or even have a voice to sing, but the Holy Spirit will have you singing. You might blast it out in the shower or in the car while you drive. But if the Holy Spirit hits you, you will sing.

Elizabeth's song is grown folk's music because she acknowledges and celebrates that Mary, a humble and confused teenager, standing before her, had been called to assume grown folk's responsibilities. She might be in a teenager's body, but being pregnant positioned her to take on grown folks' responsibilities, whether she was ready or not. Elizabeth further confirmed the radical implications of the child Mary bore. Mary's child was not a teenage inconvenience; he was a child of promise—grown folk's business.

Now you all know what happens in the church: one person, one sister, starts singing, and everybody starts singing. Mary started singing. Mary's song was composed in a grown folk's way. She was not singing the lyrics of a child or a teenager. This was no *Mary Had a Little Lamb*. Mary's song was grown folk's music. **I believe we can offer up a proposal for Christmas 2023. We can propose that Mary's song is a song of the liberation lyrics of grown folks. It is an invitation for us to consider the implications of a grown-up Christmas.** Just as Mary had to grow up, her song invites us to evolve from a child-centered understanding of Christmas to a grown-up understanding of Christmas.

ALVIN: Perhaps it might be helpful if we share with our sisters and brothers what we're talking about when we speak of grown folks' music. For me, grown folks' music is songs of maturity that speak to the complex challenges of life, while at the same time providing a voice to say what needs to be said. I have some more, but what do you have?

DIANA: When I think of grown folks' music, I think of music that touches the very depths of our souls. As a little girl, I can remember sitting next to my mother in church. Every time someone sang *Amazing Grace*, there was something about the lyrics of that song that brought up some of the complex challenges she was facing in life, but at the same time, assured her that God was aware.

ALVIN: I see how this perspective of grown folks' music helps us with Christmas. Most of us have a child-centered understanding of Christmas, and consider our best Christmases were when we were children. I did love most of my childhood Christmases, nor do I desire to diminish the unbridled joyfulness of childhood. I loved the joyful pageantry of Christmas, anticipating what I might get, going to sleep early, and waking up early to unwrap presents. I even enjoyed counting down the days to Christmas. It was a lot of fun. I enjoyed trying to make Christmas fun for my children, too. But, I haven't been a child for a long time, so at 72 years old. My age and life experiences force me to join with Paul who said *"When I was a child I spoke like a child, acted like a child, but when I became a mature person/grown up"* [I'm supposed] *to put away childish things."*

For Christmas to grow up, we need to grow up. We need to grow beyond the self-centered tendencies of our Christmas celebrations and, like Mary, embrace a liberation song. Christmas will never grow up if people stay stuck in childhood. Here we are still getting mad when things don't go our way. We cancel out people who make mistakes or even hurt us. That's childish! Going out spending money we don't have on things we don't need to impress people we don't like, that's childish! Keeping ourselves as the focus of Christmas is childish.

When we grow up, our children will have a better chance of growing up and connecting their lives with causes greater than themselves. I love Christmas, but our world needs a grown-up Christmas. We need a maturity that can deliver us from material things to a spiritual outlook and make us more concerned about people. We need a Christmas that makes God's love real in the world every day, and not just one day. We need a Christmas that will make us merry all year, and not just in December.

DIANA: Oh, I love Christmas songs, but even my Christmas songs are grown folk music. I might sing some of the children's Christmas songs with children, but they do nothing to nourish my soul. I can enjoy them for a moment, but at this age, I don't have any business trying to connect what's going on in my world with any **Jingle Bells, Rudolph the Red-Nosed Reindeer, Frosty the Snowman, Santa Claus is Coming to Town, Deck the Halls, I Dream of a White Christmas, or The Twelve Days of Christmas.**

Jingle Bells won't bring justice. Rudolph, even with a red nose, won't help climate control. (Perhaps his nose is red because his allergies are bothering him from the toxins in the air.) I'm from East Oakland, and we never had a Frosty the Snowman. Furthermore, I pray the unhoused people in Oakland never see a snowman. I don't dream of a White Christmas; I pray for a Christmas where all people—Black, white, brown, yellow, straight, gay, or non-binary—experience the love of God. I do wish everyone a Merry Christmas, but I don't recommend anyone trying to shop themselves through the Twelve Days of Christmas. Most of us can't even afford one day. We need Christmas to grow up in ways that match the songs of grown folks. Let's see if Mary can help our Christmas grow up and tap us into the spirit of grown folks' music. Mary's song helps Christmas to grow up by showing us that grown folks' music deals with what's **real, relevant, and reliable**.

DIANA: What's Real (vss. 46-49)

Dropping into our text, Mary says, "My soul magnifies the Lord and my spirit rejoices." These are grown folk lyrics. The Message Bible says Mary is bursting with good news! That's because Mary is singing about God's goodness and about what God has done for her. Mary is singing because God sees her—a poor, marginalized, invisibilized, silenced teenage girl. Mary gives attention to what God is doing in her life, saying, "I may be the most fortunate woman in the world, and what God has done for me will never be forgotten." Then, watch this: she directs our attention back to God. She keeps the focus on God. That's real.

Her soul is magnified. Her soul is made large because she magnified God. When the late Marvin Webb used to lead us in praise, he would tell us to "make God big." Christmas grows up when we make God big. It's not just about Santa Claus, Rudolf, Christmas trees, or even us. Get yourself off the front page. Christmas grows up when we keep the focus on God.

ALVIN: Relevant (vss. 50-53)

Mary also helps us see how Christmas grows up by demonstrating that grown folks' music is relevant because God is always relevant. Notice in the text, she speaks of the grown folks' business of God righting the wrongs in the world. God shows up and addresses the things that keep grown folks up at night—grown folks' stuff. She speaks of the things that have us looking at the news, the *Situation Room*, the *Last Word*, and even *Morning Joe*. She speaks of the things that have us turning the pages of newspapers or scrolling the screens of our devices.

These are grown folks' lyrics: "*His mercy is for those who fear him from generation to generation. [51]He has shown strength with his arm; he has scattered the proud in the thoughts of their hearts. [52]He has brought down the powerful from their thrones, and lifted up the lowly; [53]he has filled the hungry with good things, and sent the rich away empty.*"

Mary's song gives voice to the relevant issues that oppressed people have to deal with. Like a liberation theologian, she understands that God is on the side of the oppressed. God has sided with the poor. God despises the proud and mighty and has been known to bring down those who lift themselves up and lift up those who've been brought down. This is grown folks' music! She gave voice to God's involvement in a world where, like we saw on the Gilman Street exit just yesterday, a grown man and his wife with three children, holding up a sign. Grown folks' music doesn't fantasize about a red-nosed reindeer or dashing through the snow. It speaks to the relevant issues of the day with a faith perspective of God making everything all right.

DIANA – Reliable (vss.54-55):
And finally, Christmas grows up by demonstrating that grown folks' music keeps our focus on what's reliable. Using the Message Bible, Mary says God did exactly what God promised. Mary looked beyond herself to demonstrate that God sees us, that God cares, and that we can depend on God because God is a reliable God who keeps his promises.

The song concludes by citing, **"He has helped his servant Israel, in remembrance of his mercy, as he spoke to our fathers, to Abraham and to his offspring forever."** God remains faithful. God will watch over you and keep you, and God will meet all your needs. Like Lou Rawls, we might be living in a world of trouble (Rawls, 1963), but in God, you can find peace, even when we mess up. We can confess that God is reliable and faithful to forgive us. Our reliable God promises to guide us. "Trust in the Lord with all your heart, and lean not on your own understanding." Lean on God, and God will straighten out your path. When you are weary, God promises comfort, and when you are weary, God will restore you and make you strong. Oh, that's a grown folks' God, a reliable God we can depend on!

Christmas grows up when we focus on what it says about God's reliability. Last Sunday, Jimmy hustled up a choir and they sang, "Emmanuel." Emmanuel means God with us. Christmas grows up with Emmanuel. There are a number of Christmas songs that are grown folks' music and highlight the reliability of God. Let's point out a few.

ALVIN: "O Holy Night"
Context: *O Holy Night* was written in 1847 in France. The song's theme of divine light shining in the midst of darkness is grown folks' music. It resonated with the social and political upheaval of the time, including the ongoing struggle for social justice and the quest for spiritual renewal in the face of adversity. Grown folks' music!

DIANA: Joy to the World"

Context: Written in 1719 by Isaac Watts, *Joy to the World* is grown folks' music. It captures the anticipation of the arrival of God's kingdom on earth. Its message of joy and salvation reflects a longing for the restoration of justice and righteousness, addressing the social and spiritual challenges of the early 18th century. Grown folks' music!

DIANA: "I'll Be Home for Christmas" is grown folks' music. It's a Christmas song that was written during World War II, the war of our fathers. Its social context is deeply intertwined with the experiences of soldiers, civilians, and families during the human devastations of war. Grown folks' music!

ALVIN: "We Three Kings"

Context: *We Three Kings* was composed in 1857. Its portrayal of the Magi's journey to witness the birth of Jesus is saturated with imagery of justice, humility, and divine revelation. The song's themes resonate with the ethical and social consciousness of the mid-19th century, reflecting a yearning for spiritual transformation and societal renewal. Grown folks' music!

DIANA: "Jesus, O What a Wonderful Child" is grown folk's music. Its lyrics reflect the hopeful aspirations of a people whose national hymn spoke of hopes unborn having died. Yet, they sang of new hopes, new joy to all who sing glory to the newborn king.

ALVIN & DIANA: "Go Tell It on the Mountain"

Context: This is an African-American spiritual that emerged during the era of slavery in the United States. It conveys the message of liberation, drawing inspiration from the biblical narrative of Christ's birth while serving as a coded expression of resistance and hope for emancipation among enslaved African Americans. Grown folks' music! We invite you, Bethlehem, to grow up with Christmas and sing grown folks' music!

So let's:

> Go, tell it on the mountain
> Over the hills and everywhere
> Go, tell it on the mountain
> That Jesus Christ is born

DISCUSSION QUESTIONS

1. Describe ways in which the experience of Christmas has matured in your life.
2. What about Christmas have you left in your childhood?
3. How have you interpreted traditional Christmas songs?
4. Does Christmas move you to sing? If so, what are some of your favorite songs?

Chapter 9

THE FIFTH SAYING OF MARY: WHEN MARY FINDS US

Preached the Fifth Sunday of Advent 2023
Reverend Alvin C. Bernstine

The Theological Category: *Mariology of Search & Presence*

The Homiletical: Mary's anxious search for Jesus becomes a theology of accountability in absence. Her persistence calls communities to notice who is missing and to be restored through presence.

TEXT: *"⁴¹Now every year his parents went to Jerusalem for the festival of the Passover. ⁴² And when he was twelve years old, they went up as usual for the festival. ⁴³ When the festival was ended and they started to return, the boy Jesus stayed behind in Jerusalem, but his parents did not know it. ⁴⁴ Assuming that he was in the group of travelers, they went a day's journey. Then they started to look for him among their relatives and friends. ⁴⁵ When they did not find him, they returned to Jerusalem to search for him. ⁴⁶ After three days, they found him in the temple, sitting among the teachers, listening to them and asking them questions. ⁴⁷ And all who heard him were amazed at his understanding and his answers.⁴⁸ When his parents saw him, they were astonished; and his mother said to him, "Child, why have you treated us like this? Look, your father and I have been searching for you in great anxiety." ⁴⁹He said to them, "Why were you searching for me? Did you not know that I must be in my Father's house?" 50 But they did not understand what he said to them. ⁵¹ Then he went down with them and came to Nazareth, and was obe-*

dient to them. His mother treasured all these things in her heart. [52] *And Jesus increased in wisdom and in years, and in divine and human favor. (Luke 2:41-52, NRSV)*

Questions About This Odd Text

I have many questions about this odd text
Where the soon-to-be teenager's parents were vexed
By the child who went off and then worried them sick,
And they scratched their heads, saying, "What makes this boy tick?"

Oh, why did they travel e'en just for a day,
While they thought with the neighbors he'd be on their way?
And I wonder just where for three days did he stay?
Did he sleep? Did he eat? Did he ever once play?
(Scott L. Barton, Textweek, 2015)

This is, indeed, an odd text. Yet, what makes it odder is how one of the major characters who speaks has historically been minimized, invisibilized, and silenced. In our text, Mary, an adult, a colonized and traumatized mother, has more to say than Jesus, but her words are eclipsed by the words of a twelve-year-old. Perhaps it has to do with Mary's position in our doctrines and teaching, or perhaps it has something to do with the longstanding patriarchal blind spots of the Protestant church.

Consider the Catholic church. The Catholic church positioned Mary in a lofty place. She is considered the Mother of God. There are several prayers to Mary, one of which is the Hail Mary:

"Hail Mary, full of grace, the Lord is with thee; blessed art thou among women and blessed is the fruit of thy womb, Jesus. Holy Mary, Mother of God, pray for us sinners, now and at the hour of our death. Amen.

There are even rosary beads designated to Mary where the rosary states, **"Hail Mary! Hail Mary! Hail Mary!"** But Protestants, including good Baptists, have not honored Mary as such. We respect her as Jesus's mother, but we have never positioned her in a lofty place, let alone consider her as Mother of God, or an active agent of salvation and liberation. Yet, even as Jesus's mother, she has not been uniquely revered, honored, or respected. For the most part, she's been a cute little doctrinal sidebar or someone we use to decorate our Nativity scenes, and she might be mentioned during the Seven Last Words.

What if we opened our hearts to the importance of Mary as essential to understanding Jesus? What if we allowed ourselves an opportunity to see Mary as essential to the gospel story? How much different our own sense of discipleship might be if Mary became a functional person, not just a cute sidebar or a prop in the manger scene? Perhaps we might discover in Mary some powerful tools to make the gospel more real if we position ourselves to be found by Mary.

Luke's gospel helps us by including this story about Mary's persistence in finding her lost son. In the story, Jesus was not home alone, having been inadvertently separated from his family. He was supposed to be in the caravan leaving Jerusalem, going back to Nazareth. No one knew where he was. Mary led the effort to find him. The word in the text describes her search as she **"fervently and passionately sought"** him. Jesus used the same fervent and passionate word when he answered, "Why were you *fervently and passionately* looking for me?" **Luke's gospel suggests that when Mary finds us, we are called to give an account for our absence.** I believe that's how we shall shape this sermon. If we are truly trying to be like Jesus, we are going to need a Mary-finds-us- moment. We are going to need a moment in our lives when Mary finds us, and we are called to give an account for our absence. What else drives this part of the story is Jesus's absence. He was absent. He was not where he was supposed to be, and too often we are not where we're supposed to be. We are not where we are supposed to be for God, one another, and sometimes for ourselves. Oh yes, we can be lost to our true sense of self.

Again, Mary sought him because he was missing from the community, and she needed him to account for his absence. If we have learned anything in the last three-plus COVID-stricken years, we have learned that ministry begins with presence. After being forced into isolative spaces, we learned the value of presence. As a faith community, the Lord allowed us to even use our pandemic-stricken time to study some amazing works on how to best be present with one another. We learned that being present provides healing and new life opportunities in spaces characterized by broken communities. Ministry is an experience of presence. Love happens in experiences of presence. Healing is the response of presence, and prayer is the language of presence. With all our differences, the one thing we hold in common is a need for presence. We don't do well with absence.

This is how we enter the Jesus story around the idea of when Mary finds you. Mary responds to the absence. Mary finding us is a metaphorical response to our experiences of absence. "Mary finds us" is a biblical truth about God's concern for people who are not where they're supposed to be. What is most often overlooked in this story is that Jesus's absence disrupted the community. Mary's "mother anxiety" is understandably pronounced because Jesus was not where he was supposed to be. The emotion that drives the story and Mary's search is an ominous sense of anxiety caused by absence. The community of Jesus had just enjoyed a festive moment and was returning to their normal spaces of responsibility and interaction. While returning to the normal spaces of communal responsibility and interaction, it was discovered that Jesus was missing. An ominous sense of anxiety gripped the community because a valued person, a young man, was absent.

What makes his absence so concerning is that, according to Jewish tradition, one of the most valuable commodities to a healthy community is young males. The absence of young males disrupts community life because it places a community's future at risk. Young males symbolize hopeful possibilities. In our story, a young person, who probably had just completed his bar mitzvah—the initiation rite for male children—was missing. Interestingly, they had gone a whole day's journey before noticing that he was missing, and it took three more days to find him.

We don't have to think too hard to make a connection between this story and the state of the African American church. Black male children are missing in today's church. Sadder yet is the fact that we have been traveling on this road for much longer than a day, and no one seems to acknowledge that our communities are broken without the presence of young Black men. Our future is at risk when there are no young males in our midst. While we may not embrace Mariology like the Catholics, we need a Mary spirit to emerge and help us to bring healing and wholeness to our broken communities. We need Mary to find us.

I am personally thankful for Mary's fifth saying because it forces us to think about who's missing. For people who are concerned about bringing healing to the community, one of the most powerful questions we can ask ourselves is "Who's missing?" Who's missing in our ministries? Who's missing around the tables of our decision-making? Whose absence speaks volumes to the brokenness of our families and communities?

There's much we could say about the brokenness of our communities based on who's absent, but give me a few moments to mine the text and ponder what could happen when Mary finds us. I pray that when Mary finds us, she at least finds us in a similar position to Jesus. What did she find when she found Jesus? When Mary found Jesus, she found him in a **good place among good people, engaging in good conversation.** Thus, I suggest that when Mary finds us, I pray she finds us in **a good place, around good people, and having good conversations.**

Mary and Joseph engaged in their anxiety-filled three-day search for Jesus, and the only specific place the text tells us they searched was among family and friends. If I were searching for a 12-year-old boy, the first place I would look would be among family and friends. Yet, the story informs us he was not among family and friends. He was not hanging out with Cousin John or sleeping over in Auntie Elizabeth's wagon. When they couldn't locate him among family and friends, they returned to Jerusalem. They went back to the big city—the festival town and a dangerous place. In Jerusalem, they searched fervently and passionately for three days.

We are not told where they searched. My sanctified imagination and experience as a parent of marginalized children lead me to believe that they first spent time searching in some of the worst places. They probably went to the busy boulevards of commerce. They possibly searched in places where no twelve-year-old needs to be, such as the red light district, on a corner of confusion, or hanging around the liquor store. They had to at least go by the Jerusalem Police Department, and possibly, the Roman Sheriff's Department. Momma had to check the hospital and Jerusalem Juvenile Hall. Perhaps they even went by the city morgue and looked at unidentified corpses.

After three days of searching, only God knows when they went to the Temple. **They finally went to a good place.** I don't know why we parents always begin thinking the worst before we ever consider the best. Perhaps anxiety defaults the mind to think the worst. Yet, they ended up at a good place.

They went to the place where praise songs were sung, scriptures read, testimonies given, and prayers offered. Something shifted in Mary's search from a fatalistic mentality and looking in bad places to a faith mentality, and she went to a good place.

I pray when Mary finds us, and those who are missing among us, she finds us in a good place. I pray she finds us in the place where praise songs are being sung, scriptures read, testimonies given, and prayers offered. If not in the Lord's house, I pray Mary finds us somewhere where people are being edified, where dreams are being materialized, and hopes are realized.

In 1992, when I was transitioning from Nashville to New York, the National Baptist Convention met in Manhattan. And like Stevie Wonder's **"Living Just Enough for the City,"** one of my best friends and I fixed our minds on getting into some non-Baptist mischief. However, before we did anything, we visited the Saint Patrick's Cathedral. Sitting in the awesomeness of that grand sanctuary, with images of Mary in stained glass splendor, the Spirit of God cleansed our minds of all thoughts of mischief. Mary found us in a good place and made sure we got back to where we were supposed to be.

Oh, I pray that when Mary finds us—the people of the marginalized, disenfranchised, invisibilized, and demonized—she finds us in a good place.

Secondly, **I pray that when Mary finds us, like Jesus, she finds us among some good people.** For three days, possibly searching in bad places among bad people, they ended up in a good place among good people. The Bible says, "They found Jesus among the teachers, some good people." I suspect that if I came up missing and my absence broke the community, the last place my anxious Momma would have looked for me was among teachers. If truth be told, I doubt my mother knew the names of all my teachers at the school, and she certainly didn't know all of my teachers at the University of Hard Times and in the College of Hard Knocks. She couldn't have known that some of my best teachers were hustlers, drug dealers, fast women, and money-grabbing merchants. They taught me much about what I didn't want to do and what I didn't want to be. I was blessed to find some good people in bad places, and much to my dismay, I've encountered some bad people in good places.

Mary and Joseph found Jesus among good people—the church folks. Please know that I'm not so naïve that I believe all church people are good people, but the Lord knows there are some good people in the Lord's church. Some of the best people in the world are church folks. They might not be known to teach, or even be part of the teaching ministry, but some of the best people are in the church. Some of God's best people are in the Ushers' Ministry, the Deacons' Ministry, the Trustees' Ministry, the Preaching Ministry, and the Culinary Ministry. We might have to first go among the other people, but I pray that when Mary finds us, she finds us among some good people. One of my life's goals is based upon the discovery that there are some good people in the world, and I'm doing all I can to be one of them.

Finally, **I pray that when Mary finds us, she finds us engaging in good conversations.** When

Mary found Jesus, he was in a good place among good people with his mind on good things. The Bible says, **"After three days, they found him in the temple, sitting among the teachers, listening to them and asking them questions."** They found Jesus having a conversation around God-talk. He was engaged in a theological conversation, listening and asking questions.

One of the things we are made to do and will do is talk, but it's not always good conversation. If 24-hour news has taught us anything, it has taught us that bad talk, gossip, negative talk, destructive talk, criticizing talk, judgmental talk, and even hateful talk sells. However, they found Jesus engaging in good conversation. I don't know what he asked, but he certainly explored the meaning of scripture and its relevance for the day. He probably wanted to know how the people of God had become a colony of Rome. He certainly asked about why good people suffer and evil prosper. He had to ask a few questions about justice and the hopeless plight of the least of these. He had to ask a question or two about the goodness of the Lord in a world marked by oppression and Jewish exploitation.

When Mary found Jesus, he was engaged in good conversation because the Bible says, *"All who heard him were amazed at his understanding and his answers."* I pray that when Mary finds us, she finds us in good conversations. I pray she finds us engaged in conversations about the goodness of the Lord in the land of the living. I pray she finds us in conversations about justice, freedom, and equality. I pray Mary finds us in conversations that build up people, love on people, and see the good in people, and the possibilities in people. I pray Mary finds us talking positively about the Lord's church, encouraging the Pastor and leadership. I pray Mary finds us engaging in conversations of strategies to make God's love real in the world.

I don't know about you, but I pray God finds us in a good place, among good people, engaging in good conversations, so that Mary can do for us what she did with Jesus. The Bible says that although she did not understand everything he was talking about, *"His mother treasured all these things in her heart. And Jesus increased in wisdom and in stature and in favor with God and man."*

I pray that when Mary finds us, she will do for us what we've not done for her. She will hold us in her heart, and love on us, giving us grace to increase in wisdom and stature and in favor with God and our brothers and sisters.

DISCUSSION QUESTIONS

1. What space does Mary hold in your life?
2. How has Mary's voice been silenced in your faith tradition?
3. Who are the people missing in your faith community?
4. If Mary were to find you, where would you be?
5. If Mary were to find you, what would you be talking about?

Chapter 10

THE SIXTH SAYING OF MARY:
A Heart for More in 2024

Preached on the First Sunday of 2024, January 7
Reverend Alvin C. Bernstine

The Theological Category: *Mariology of Abundance*

The Homiletical Frame: Mary's words at Cana embody a theology of open-heartedness in scarcity. Her heart for more resists deficit-thinking and anticipates joy as God's provision.

TEXT: *On the third day, there was a wedding in Cana of Galilee, and the mother of Jesus was there. ² Jesus and his disciples had also been invited to the wedding. ³ When the wine gave out, the mother of Jesus said to him, "They have no wine." ⁴ And Jesus said to her, "Woman, what concern is that to me and to you? My hour has not yet come. (John 2:1-4, NRSV)*

And when they wanted wine, the mother of Jesus is saying to him, "They have no wine." (John 2:3, Greek Text)

"When the wine gave out, the mother of Jesus said to him, "They have no wine." (John 2:3, NRSV)

A good start lays a solid foundation for success. How we start says much about how we will end. A bad start doesn't necessarily mean a bad end, nor does a good one guarantee a good ending. Many bad starts have ended incredibly well, and many good starts have ended badly. However, there are a few things we do want to start well. Two of which grab our attention in the text today. Unless you are a perpetual hater or eternal pessimist, we all want marriages and New Year's to get off to a good start. Anyone who has ever married or loved someone who got married usually anticipated a great start. The honeymoon is, in fact, a celebration of a good start. Likewise, we habitually extend a Happy New Year to people, and we go into a New Year with the belief that it will be a Happy New Year. This year, thanks to a sister we met at Yoshi's, I modified my New Year's greeting, and I'm praying that we have a "Happier New Year!"

The setting of our text, which becomes in the Gospel of John, the place of Jesus's first miracle or sign, is a marriage. We are not told who the wedding was for. We don't have the name of the bride or the groom. We are not told who the marrying couple was related to or their connection in the community. What seems most important for us to know is simply that it's a marriage—a gathering of people celebrating love, lifting up hopefulness, and well wishes for abundant future success and family blessings. Also, in the first verse, the author clues us in by telling us something of utmost importance. It tells us: ***"And the mother of Jesus was there.***

Interestingly, Mary's name is not even mentioned. If it weren't for Matthew and Luke, we would not know her name because John never mentions it. There's a wedding in Cana of Galilee, and Mary, Jesus's mother, is there. The text adds, ***"Jesus also was invited to the wedding with his disciples."*** The bride and groom are there. Family members are there. Their people are there. Mary is there. Jesus and his disciples are there. The community is there, and according to Jewish custom, the seven-day wedding celebration is three days in. By verse 3, we have a problem. The text says, **"When the wine ran out …"** One text says, ***"When the wine gave out …"*** The Greek translation of the text exacerbated the situation by saying, ***"When they wanted wine, the mother of Jesus said to him (Jesus), 'They have no wine.'"***

I know most of you are Kool-Aid drinkers, soda water sippers, juicers, and committed to non-alcoholic beverages, but in the first and twenty-first century Jewish wedding, there is no celebration without wine. Wine makes the celebration! It is essential to every meaningful celebration. Wine represents joy and stimulates joyfulness. Wine enriches socialization. People are more likely to talk to one another, dance, and laugh when they have wine. But more importantly, it symbolizes blessings, joyfulness, transformation, and sacred covenant-making. To not have wine is like Billy Preston's

"A song with no melody,

dance with no steps

Or a story with no moral.

Will it go round in a circle?"

To have no wine is a wedding symbolic of a marriage with no love.

We know that wine is made from grapes, and just as grapes must be processed into wine, the bride and the groom must be processed from single life into married life. Moreover, it was an embarrassment to have people in a space of joyful new beginnings and lack the one thing that most symbolized it. A wedding with no wine represented a serious social, economic, and even spiritual deficit. You can have a so-so wedding dress, a rented tuxedo, second-hand wedding rings, a nasty cake, tacky bridesmaids and groomsmen, but not to have wine was a wedding disaster!

You could even have a sorry band, singing songs that you don't ever sing at a wedding, like:

- Bon Jovi: **"You Give Love a Bad Name"**
- Whitney Houston: **"It's Not Right, But It's Okay"**
- Ernie K. Doe: **"Mother In-Law"**
- Kanye West: **"Gold Digger"**
- Gladys Knight and the Pips: **"It Should Have Been Me"**
- Beyonce: **"Single Ladies"**
- Temptations: **"Just My Imagination"**

To have no wine is a serious deficit, a shameful scarcity, and an embarrassing state of neediness. But everything changes because the Bible says Mary, *"the mother of Jesus was there."* Mary allows us to see the transformative power of an open heart. What puts Mary in the story is that, in a moment of embarrassing neediness, she has a heart for more. Mary's heart addresses shameful scarcity because she has a heart for more, even in the context of embarrassing shortages. **The sixth saying of Mary offers us a powerful example of someone who had a heart for more. In spaces of known need and severe lack, Mary teaches us how to show up with a heart for more.** She helps us to see that no material lack needs to diminish our hearts.

What makes this story and our theme so relevant for people walking into a New Year is that too many of us have allowed deficits and shortages to define us. We use what we don't have, our deficits and lack, to describe us. What embarrasses them identifies us. We will never have a Happy New Year, or "happy" anything else, as long as our hearts are set on scarcity. Once we internalize deficits, our hearts shrink, and we define who we are based on what we don't have.

We set ourselves up for unhappiness as long as we focus on what we don't have. You show me a fight, a war even, and I'll show you some people focused on what they don't have, trying to take from other folks who don't have. America claims to be the greatest country in the world, but it has closed its heart on what once was its defining creed:

"Give me your tired, your poor, your huddled masses yearning to breathe free, the wretched refuse of your teeming shore. Send these, the homeless, tempest-tossed to me, I lift my lamp beside the golden door!"

I've been around the church most of my life and heard Bible and songs about:

"Our God shall provide our needs according to his riches and glory."

"And God is able to bless you abundantly, so that in all things at all times, having all that you need, you will abound in every good work."

"I have come that you may have life and have it more abundantly."

Give, and it will be given to you. A good measure, pressed down, shaken together and running over, will be poured into your lap. For with the measure you use, it will be measured to you."

Every Sunday, someone says, *"Bring the tithes into the storehouse that there may be food in my house. And thereby test me, says the Lord of hosts, 'if I will not open up the windows of heaven and pour you out a blessing that there will not be room enough to receive it.'"*

However, I've yet to sit in a church meeting and someone show up with a Mary-sized heart who believes that just because we don't have, doesn't mean we can't have. Most church meetings are diminished because some scarcity-minded person, or group, thinks it their sanctified responsibility to bring up what we don't have. You're talking about a "Hail Mary!" when what was scheduled to be a celebration of new beginnings became a scene of embarrassing desperation. Yet Mary, with a heart for more, kept the party going. I know we tend to focus on what Jesus did, but Jesus did not do anything until Mary interceded. Mary helps us to see that our heart space shapes our reality, not the deficits in our lives, or the world. Our hearts are more than life's deficits. A big heart overcomes life's deficits.

This is no new reality to us. Think about it! In enslavement, we had a heart for freedom. In injustice, we had a heart for justice. In inequality, we had a heart for equality. In sexism, we had a heart for inclusion. In the brokenness of biases, we had a heart for healing and wholeness. Mary shows up in a space of lack and need and speaks from a heart of abundance.

As we enter into this New Year, someone needs to be asking how do we cultivate a heart for more in 2024? I've shared with you a 24-day devotional that I pray represents the heart of Mary. Mary enlarges our hearts for more by demonstrating at least three things: **presence, perspective, and petition.** Mary demonstrates to us that a heart for more is about **remaining present, having perspective, and actively petitioning.**

To have a heart for more in 2024, Mary teaches us how presence cultivates heart space. The more present we are, the larger our hearts become. The Bible says the mother of Jesus was there because she really was there. She was present. She was not just on the premises; she was in the space.

Mary wasn't like some of us. When she caught wind that they had a wine shortage problem, she didn't say it was time to get out of here. She didn't allow the deficits of the situation to disconnect her from the moment. As a result of her remaining present, we are privileged to see the bigness of her heart.

After nearly 72 years of life, 47 years of preaching and 40 as a pastor, I want to confess something that I now regret. I spent a great deal of my early ministry being on premises but not in the spaces. I allowed my fears, insecurities, shame, and anxieties to separate me from whatever was going on by always reading a book. I disconnected from people by hiding in books. Consequently, I not only closed my heart to what was going on in the lives of other people, but I deprived myself of meaningful relationships. Forgive me if you find me overdoing it sometimes. I'm trying to make up for the time I lost by not being present.

Mary remained fully present to the happenings of the house, which enabled her to hear, feel, sense, and most importantly, empathize. Her heart was where she was. She did not have a divided heart. Because she captured the mood of the house, she was able to shape a perspective for the good of the house.

Secondly, Mary helps us to have a heart for more because being present gave her perspective. Perspective is about seeing, and how we see is shaped by our hearts. Yes, Mary saw a celebration turned into desperation, but she didn't allow the developing mood to close her heart.

Too many of us allow social moods to shape our hearts. For instance, the dominant mood of our country is that we don't have enough for everybody. Therefore, the white people need to look after the white people, the black people the black people, the Asians the Asians, the Jews the Jews, the Republicans the Republicans, and the Democrats the Democrats. Such a mood gets in the way of the lofty perspective of being the United States of America. How can we ever be united when our dominant mood divides us? Our mood limits our perspective, and our limited perspective closes our hearts.

Mary understood the potential of the wine shortage getting in the way of a celebration, as well as its impact upon the future of the bride and groom. Yet, because she possessed perspective, she was able to envision another outcome. She saw the possibility of something new and something better, even during announced shortages. Her heart opened for more by expanding her imagination, and her imagination moved her to petition. She went to Jesus. She didn't know what he was going to do. He had never responded to a wine shortage before, nor had he yet turned a bag lunch of a hungry boy into a buffet for a famished multitude. She didn't know how he was going to address the shortage. All she knew was that her heart told her to go to Jesus.

This is exciting! Mary's petition came in four words, *"They have no wine."* She didn't write out a long prayer list or give him a variety of reasons why the wine shortage was his business. In fact, he seemed to suggest that the wine shortage was not his business. He didn't really even understand why Mary was all concerned and into other people's business. He curtly responded, *"Woman, what concern is that to me and to you?"*

Someone needs to hear me today; 2024 is here. We are here. Our folks are here. The shortages are here, and we've heard many reasons why it won't get better. Many of us have internalized the community-destroying ethic of "Mind your own business and leave mine alone." Mary's sixth saying challenges us to cultivate our hearts by petitioning Jesus. Jesus said, **"Whatever you ask in my name shall be given to you."** She petitioned Jesus. Someone once said, "The problem with Christianity is that no one has ever truly tried it." We've talked about it. We've sung about it. We even preached about it. Yet very few of us have tried it.

Being a Christian is not about church, denominations, creeds, doctrines, or traditions. Being a follower of Jesus means believing that, whatever is going on in our lives, he can fix it. Whatever deficits we are facing, he can deal with them. Whatever the shortages of life, his grace is sufficient. I love the way Mary petitioned Jesus. She just told him the need. They didn't have the one thing necessary to celebrate a new beginning. They didn't have the one thing needed for a community to celebrate God doing a new thing. It wasn't money, clothes, a job, or a new car. They didn't have any joy!

Joy changes everything! Joy turns a bad situation into a good situation. Joy will make you happy even when you ought to be sad. Joy will pick you up, and joy will turn you around.

No wonder Jesus said, *"The joy I give you the world can't take away."*

I can appreciate more the Christmas song that says:

> Joy to the world, the Lord is come!
>
> Let Earth receive her King!
>
> The glory of His righteousness,
>
> Let heaven and nature sing.

Thank God for Mary because Mary knew who to go to when joy was being challenged by a scarcity spirit.

DISCUSSION QUESTIONS

1. How do deficits shape your life?
2. How do deficits shape the life of your church?
3. What would change for you if you possessed a Mary-sized heart?
4. What does being present mean to you?
5. In moments of scarcity, who do you consult first?
6. Describe a moment in your life, or the life of your family, or church, where the presence of joy made a difference.

Chapter 11

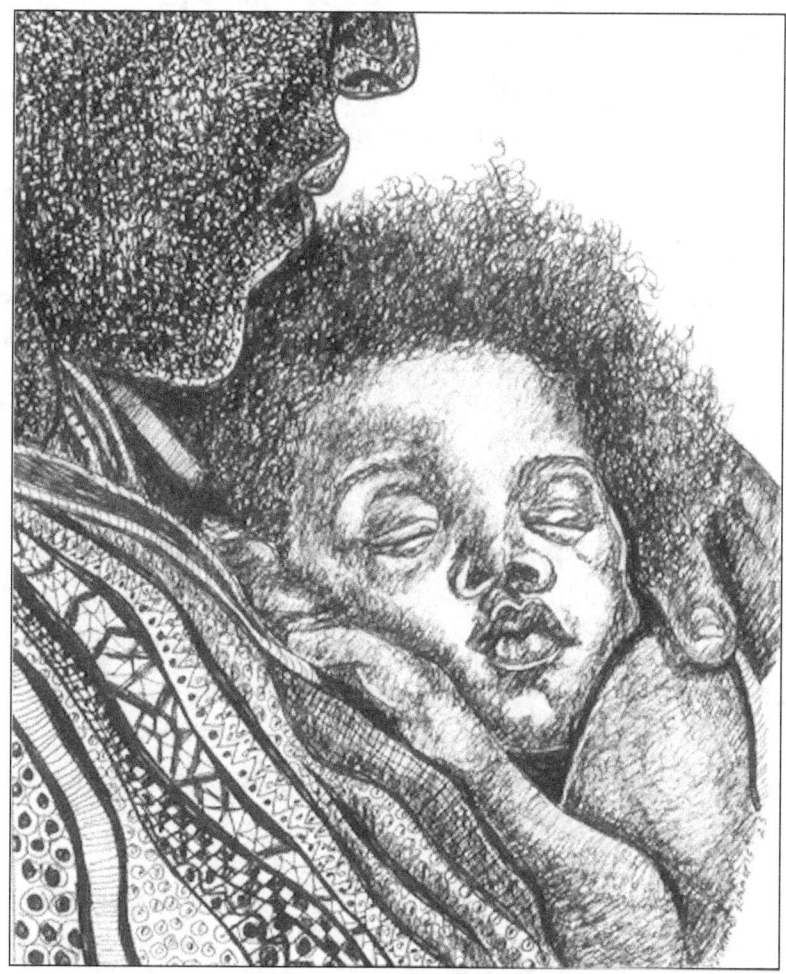

THE SEVENTH SAYING OF MARY (John 2:5)
"What Mama Said"

January 14, 2024
Reverend Diana Becton

The Theological Category: *Mariology of Obedience*

The Homiletical Frame: Mary's final recorded words are a theology of comprehensive, urgent obedience. Her maternal authority insists that miracles depend on doing what Jesus says.

His mother said to the servants, "Do whatever he tells you." (John 2:5 NRSV)

Today, we explore the seventh saying of Mary, and please note that this seventh saying is also the last time Mary speaks in the Bible. Yet, her final words speak volumes to us today when she says, "Do whatever he tells you." Thus, I want to talk today about "What Mama Said."

Without question, words from our mothers are memorable. For instance, during my early adult years, Mama would often painfully look at me and say, "All your sense is bought and paid for." It was Mama's way of saying that along my journey from childhood to adulthood, I didn't always listen or heed to her advice. She would speak, warn, and advise, but I just wouldn't listen. I would do what I wanted to do the way I wanted to do it, as if Mama never spoke, or worse yet, as if her words never meant anything.

My Mama was a praying Mama. Mama tried her best to steer me in the right direction, but I wanted to do things my way. And because I did not listen to what Mama said, I had to learn life's lessons the hard way. Mama was right. All my sense is bought and paid for I painfully matriculated in the College of Hard Knocks and did graduate studies at the University of Hard Times. Looking back, I wish I had listened to what Mama said. Especially when, in her soothing soft voice, she would say, "Chile, I' am your mother, I won't say anything to hurt you."

I should have listened to what my praying Mama said because she had been through some things. During the Great Migration, she was among the millions of Black people who moved from the South to escape racial violence, in search of relief from the oppression of the Jim Crow South. Mama left all that was familiar to pursue economic and educational opportunities in an unfamiliar place. Mama went through many trials and tribulations that she didn't want me to have to suffer. When she gave advice, something should have gone off in my head that said, "Just do it." I should have listened to what Mama said. (I should have a few more witnesses in the room or on Zoom.)

Dropping into our text, we encounter Mary at a wedding in the small town of Cana. Mary, the Mother of Jesus, is there, as well as Jesus and his disciples. We don't know how long the wedding festivities had been going on, but weddings typically included the whole town and usually lasted up to seven days. Through the attentive witness of Mary, we learn that during the wedding, a serious problem emerged. The wine ran out. Pastor Bernstine elaborated last week on the staggering crisis of a wedding with no wine. At a big Jewish wedding, there is no party spirit without wine. Wine is an essential part of the feast, and it is deemed necessary for a joyous occasion. Everybody feels joyful and happy when the wine is flowing. Moreover, wine symbolized the sacred and abundant blessings of God upon the marriage. Running out of wine could have been a serious embarrassment for the hosts. To have no wine at a wedding was a serious problem.

Mary took this serious problem to Jesus, saying, "There is no wine," and then watch this: Even though Mary had no idea what Jesus might say or do, she turned to the servants and said, "Do whatever he tells you." Clearly, Mary understood that *new life possibilities can happen when we listen to what a praying Mama says.* She told the servants, "*Whatever he says, do it!*

Mary does not ask Jesus to make, buy, or create more wine. She simply takes her concern to Jesus and entreats the servants to do whatever he says. I'm intrigued by Mary's words. Her words expose a faith perspective that could help us today. Most of us pray. We do pray. We do take our problems to Jesus, but then, watch this; we also include our pre-packaged notions and assumptions of what the outcome should be. We present the problem, but then we start telling Jesus what to do about it, and how we think it ought to be worked out.

We are not told that the servants had any opinions about how to deal with the crisis at hand. Yet, Mary's direct orders insinuate that they might have had some. If they were anything like us, opinions abounded, some more helpful than others. Somebody probably said, "Let's pass the hat and help out. Let's do a fundraiser! We don't have a lot of time, but put up a FUNDME page." Someone had to say, "Let's call the liquor store or the winery and make an emergency take-out order." Let's see if DoorDash or Grubhub can deliver. The naysayers had to say, "Shame on them, trying to have a wedding without wine. I knew that boy and girl weren't ready to get married. Let's leave and find something else to do with our time."

It is just like when, as a child, I didn't listen to what Mama said; today, some of us don't want to do what Jesus says. The Bible says, "Walk by faith and not by sight," "Trust in the Lord and don't lean on your own understanding," and "With God all things are possible," even a good wedding. We have yet to learn how to get ourselves out of the way, turn our concerns over to Jesus, and do whatever he tells us to do. Whatever he says, do it!

How might we learn from the power of Mary's words: "Whatever he says, just do it"? I think Mary would sum it up around two words: obedience and urgency. Obedience is about surrender. It is the surrender of our will and way to the will and ways of God. It is our surrendering any claims on how a thing should be done, as well as the outcome. It is us letting go and getting out of the way, so God can rule the day. If we nuance obedience with the words of Mary, obedience ought to have a comprehensive understanding and then an urgent response.

Comprehensive Understanding of Obedience

Mary said, "Do whatever he tells you to do." Whatever is an all-inclusive word. It is vast and broad. It means all things, anyone and everything, and everyone. No limits, no boundaries, no exceptions. Do anything and everything Jesus commands you to do. It's about walking in obedience, unhindered by our views and perspectives. Obedience must be approached with a comprehensive understanding that it includes everything, all things, and anything. Perhaps comparing insurance coverages, liability versus comprehensive, might help us. Liability insurance covers other folks but not me. I can lose everything, including my life, and get nothing. Comprehensive insurance covers me and everybody else.

When the wine ran out at the wedding in Cana, everything depended on whether the servants obeyed and their understanding of obedience. It covered their words and their actions. When Jesus gave instructions to the servants, they did not know what would happen next, but they obeyed. They had no clue what would happen; they just did what they were told to do. They put 20 to 30 gallons of water into the water jars without an inkling of what would happen next, and they certainly did not know what Jesus would do. Jesus was about to turn water into wine, but everything depended on the servant's obedience. Everything depended on the servants being obedient and not allowing their ideas and views to limit their actions. Obedience, no matter how unusual the instructions they were given. And make no mistake, the instructions were unusual. Think about it, there was no wine, and they were told to get some water.

Now, this is not the first time people have received unusual instructions. Moses put the blood of the lamb on the doorposts to save Black lives, because Black Lives Matter. Naaman, dipped seven times in the Jordan and was healed. Joshua marched around the walls of Jericho and gave a shout, and the walls came tumbling down. Ruth trusted in the Lord and left her home. Deborah trusted the Lord to give her army the victory when no man had the courage to even fight. And don't forget Mary! The instructions may sound crazy to the normal mind, but the key is to walk in comprehensive obedience to what the Lord says.

"Do whatever he tells you." Some two thousand years later, the only thing that has changed is the servants. I wonder today if there are any servants at BMBC willing to do whatever he says, even when it doesn't make sense, or compute with our predictions and calculations. Is there anyone here today willing to just do what he says? It may not be the way you or I would do it. It sure isn't the way we used to do it. But, are you willing to just do what he says?

Mary said, "Do whatever he says." Are there any servants who can testify that it doesn't sound right that after you lose your job to be told to be at peace? It doesn't make sense when the doctor gives you a bad report, but you are told to maintain faith. It makes no sense to trust when you have more bills than money, more problems than solutions, and more questions than answers. Comprehensive obedience requires us to do whatever Jesus says, without limits or exceptions, no matter how crazy it sounds. *Comprehensive obedience.*

Prompt/Urgent Response

Don't delay. Just do it! Whatever he says, do it. Notice the urgency in Mary's words. First, when she learned of the problem, she went straight to Jesus. She didn't go to the neighbors, her girlfriend from the hood, the groom, the father of the bride, or any of the disciples. She went straight to Jesus.

Too often, we waste precious time and energy going to other folks before we go to Jesus. If our concerns are urgent, they need an urgent response. Don't waste your time texting, talking, emailing, posting on Facebook, Instagramming, X'ing, or TikToking; take the problem straight to Jesus!

Mary urgently went to Jesus and relayed her urgency to the servants. She told them, "Whatever he says, do it!" Don't linger, don't loiter, don't procrastinate. You don't even need a committee meeting, a motion, or a second; just do it. Do it when he says do it and how he says do it! And do it at the time he says do it! Move with a sense of urgency!

Now watch this! Here's your shout! Jesus responded to their urgent obedience with an urgent solution! Take it to Jesus, and he will move in ways you cannot imagine. Someone said, "God can move quicker than right now."

Meanwhile, back at the wedding, no one knew when the water turned into wine. It happened somewhere between the pouring in and the pouring out. All they knew was that it went in as water and came out as wine. It went in as one thing but came out as another thing. The water turning into overflowing wine is a sign to us of how Jesus works. He doesn't even touch the pots. He doesn't say a prayer or bless it with anointed oil.

Obeying servants prompted a miracle-working Jesus! When the servants obeyed, a miracle happened! When we obey the Lord, he gives abundantly and provides what we need. When we obey, Jesus can turn our weeping into laughter and our sorrow into joy. When we obey, Jesus takes our failures and turns them into a testimony. He takes our cries of pain and anguish and turns them into shouts of joy and praise. As Rev. Harriet Cross said, "He brings the Merlot of mindfulness, the Cabernet of kindness, and the Rose of righteousness." And he does it urgently!

Nike, once a struggling sneaker company, must have read Mary's words. For over fifty years, and with the blessing of Michael Jordan and Tiger Woods, Nike has proclaimed, "Just do it!" As a symbol, they used the angelic wing of the Greek goddess Nike, and today the Swoosh has become one of the most recognizable logos in the entire world.

Nike embraced the urgency of obedience in three simple words: *Just do it!*

Swoosh! Walk by faith; swoosh, not by sight.

Swoosh! Trust in the Lord with all your heart.

Swoosh! Follow me and I will make you fishers of men, women, and children. Just do it!

Swoosh! Love the Lord with all your hearts, all your soul, your mind and strength.

Swoosh! Jesus said, "Come to me, all who are weary and burdened." Bring your hurt, bring your sorrow, bring your pain, bring your loss, he will give you rest, just do it.

Swoosh! Just do it. Be strong and of good courage! Don't be afraid.

Swoosh! Just do it! Somebody needs to shout, "Won't he do it!"

Over a hundred and fifty years ago, a preacher walked up on a young man struggling with trusting and obeying God. As he shared his struggles with the pastor, he decided to just do it. His resolve to just do it inspired the preacher to sing:

When we walk with the Lord in the light of His Word,

What a glory He sheds on our way!

While we do His good will, He abides with us still

And with all who will trust and obey.

Trust and obey,

T'is the only way

To be happy in Jesus

T'is to trust and obey.

Oh, I wonder if in 2024, "Does the Lord have some BMBC servants who will swoosh our way by trusting and obeying?" Whatever he says, Swoosh! Just do it! Swoosh! Swoosh! Swoosh!

DISCUSSION QUESTIONS

1. What are some of the most memorable words of your mother?

2. How do you want your prayers answered?

3. How has your perspective on life challenged your acts of obedience?

4. Do you think Mary could help you with your obedience challenges? If not, why not?

5. Describe a time in your life where you obeyed God and God responded with an abundant outcome.

6. What will you do differently after this study and the sermons on Mary?

Chapter 12

A SERMONIC EPILOGUE (Not yet preached)

Reverend Alvin C. Bernstine
"The Testimony of A Great Finish"

The Theological Category: *Mariology of Resilient Presence*

The Homiletical Frame: Mary's silent endurance at the Cross is a theology of finishing faithfully. Her presence witnesses to strength in grief, the gift of community, and the courage to let go.

TEXT: *Near the cross of Jesus stood his mother, his mother's sister, Mary the wife of Clopas, and Mary Magdalene. [26] When Jesus saw his mother there, and the disciple whom he loved standing nearby, he said to her, "Woman, here is your son," [27] and to the disciple, "Here is your mother." From that time on, this disciple took her into his home."* (John 19:25-27, NIV)

A common mantra of common sense is: "It all depends on how you start." In many instances, good starts are great. Most engaged couples desire that their marriage have a great start, thus justifying the excessive expenditures of gaudy weddings. Most expectant parents desire their parenting adventures to get off to a good start, hence the spoiling of the first child. We walk into employment experiences and entrepreneurial adventures hoping to get off to a good start. And yes, even our forays into church life from new member to new ministry, we hope for a great start. When I began the pastorate at the Bethlehem Missionary Baptist Church, one of its most loving and faithful members, Deacon Jimmy Stuart, was very intentional about making sure that I, as the new pastor, "would get off to a great start."

However, we all know that great starts are no guarantee of great finishes. The statistics testify that most Black marriages end in divorce. The disproportionate number of young black men in prison gives witness that spoiled children make tragic mistakes. Many of you have your personal horror stories of good starts on jobs, only to encounter a boss from hell, and the job doesn't end well. And, the glaring emptiness of our pews declares that many who started off great in church will not necessarily end great. Yet, when we turn our attention to the Jesus story, we know it didn't start off great. Mary and Joseph's marriage didn't get off to a good start. Mary's pre-marital pregnancy wasn't a great start. It wasn't great for Mary or for Joseph. When her water broke at the Roman Internal Revenue Service and labor pains became excruciating, it was not a great start for a child's delivery. Her firstborn was birthed in a stable, surrounded by sheep and cattle. Shortly after his birth, Joseph disrupted the family's life, and they became immigrants, seeking political asylum in Egypt to save Jesus's life. During the child's transition ritual from childhood to manhood, he wandered off, causing Mary much grief and pain. It appears that raising Jesus was not an easy thing, perhaps because, as his mother, Mary did not experience a great start.

As an adult, he was a hot mess. Running around with a rowdy crowd, out in the streets preaching dangerous sermons about the Kingdom of God. He was helping other people when she needed help at home. Church folk started the plots against him, and his fickle friends would betray and desert him. He even got arrested and couldn't afford a lawyer. For in his own words, "The birds have nests and the foxes have holes, but the Son of Man has nowhere to lay his head."

He ended up getting crucified, lynched as a threat to the empire. But without a great start, Mary stuck by him all the way to his violent and bloody end. There was nothing great about the start, but when we stand with her at the crucifixion of Jesus, Mary provides a powerful testimony of a great finish. It is a testimony of a great finish to a painful and disruptive start. Thus, I propose that **Mary's presence and response offer hope for the colonized and traumatized who daily experience painful**

and disruptive starts and finishes. At Jesus's crucifixion, she did not speak a word, but her actions provided a testimony of a great finish.

When Jesus saw his mother there, and the disciple whom he loved standing nearby, he said to her, "Woman, here is your son," ²⁷ and to the disciple, "Here is your mother." From that time on, this disciple took her into his home."

Since my late-life trip to Ghana, I've become more intentional about shaping an African mind. Like the brother from my neighborhood, Sobrante Park, I encountered in an African village, now an African chieftain who testified that, "The American mind was killing me and I was saved by getting an African mind." From an African mind, I learned that when we hold our losses in painful and grievous spaces too long, we prevent our loved ones' spirits from moving on to their next assignment. Too often, we selfishly hold grief and loss in spaces of hurtfulness to the expense of not only our own healing, but also to the prevention of our beloved's continued spiritual journey. We stay in hurt as a way of remembering our loved ones, ignoring the fact that if they loved us as we claim, they would want us to move on so they can move on.

Is it no wonder that, according to the American Medical Association, over 85% of Americans are living with unresolved grief. This is astounding because it suggests that nearly nine out of the ten people we meet and know are struggling with painful finishes. If it isn't the loss of a loved one, it's the loss of a job, a marriage, or the loss of a way of life. Our American mind of obsessive and possessive individualism has us painfully holding on to grief-stricken finishes. We are unable to process grief, and such a failure keeps us stuck in grief.

The good news is that the more we follow Jesus, the more things we discover to love about him. Mary never stopped following Jesus. She didn't always understand him, nor always agreed with him, but she followed him. And if our text tells us anything, it tells us that Mary followed him all the way to the Cross. And at the Cross, she discovered another reason to keep loving him. She loved him probably more in his death than she did in life, because in his death, Jesus provided her a testimony of a great finish. From a place of agonizing grief, Mary's testimony is one of a great finish to a new life. She came to the cross broken; she left being made whole. She came overwhelmed; she left being held. She came seeing no future; she left living by faith.

Mary moved on from a bloody cross to being cared for by a loving community. She moved on to a great finish. The question before you and me is, "How can we move on and experience a great finish?" If we allow Mary's actions to speak louder than words, she can help us move from our painful experiences toward a great finish. Without ever uttering a mumbling word, Mary's testimony helps us to move on by, first of all, **being present and accepting the loss and living through the pain.** Before she moved on, the Bible gives witness to her being present. She did not run from the moment. She did not try to hide her pain or deny her loss. She did not deflect it in anger, projecting her pain upon someone else. She was there for herself. She was there as a mother for her son and as a follower of Jesus. She was at the cross and witnessed every horrifying cruelty inflicted upon him.

Too many of us run from our pain. If we don't do it physically, we do it emotionally. We turn inward, wrapped in grief. Some of us run to painkillers, drugs, and/or drinks.

America offers many escape routes from pain, from 24/7 entertainment to convenient sex. Being Black compounds our grief because we're not supposed to feel. But pain is painful, and many of us don't want anything to do with it. Not so with Mary, she was present, wholly connected to the painful and traumatic experience.

When I consider the power of Mary's presence, my mind goes to that Negro Spiritual:

Were you there when they crucified my Lord?

Were you there when they crucified my Lord?

Oh, oh, sometimes it causes me to tremble, tremble, tremble.

Were you there when they crucified my Lord?

As for all who follow Jesus, he can surprise us even in dying. Mary received a surprise while positioned around death. Jesus spoke to her: *"When Jesus saw his mother there, and the disciple whom he loved standing nearby, he said to her, 'Woman, here is your son,'* [27] *and to the disciple, 'Here is your mother.'"*

I don't know about you, but in a time of agonizing grief, I can think of nothing more assuring than for the Lord to speak to me. In my darkest hour, His voice brings light. While my heart breaks and bleeds, His voice soothes and heals. I don't mean any harm, but like Mary, I'd rather hear life-giving words from a dying Savior than empty words from so-called friends.

Mary's testimony of a great finish is to accept the gifts death offers. No death leaves us without giving us something. When my father died, I received the gift of his strength. Throughout his illness, Daddy never complained. I was at Momma's bedside when she breathed her last breath. As agonizing as that moment was, Momma gifted me. She gifted me with her witness that we fall down, but we get up. I learned from my mother that mistakes are not final, and there are always people in our lives who love us no matter what.

Jesus was dying, but not before he gifted Mary with a continued connection. He connected her with whom he was connected. He didn't just give her to anyone. No! The Bible identified him as the disciple whom Jesus loved. Our testimony to a great finish is to connect with those whom Jesus loves. Some of the best church folks I know are those who connected with the church following the death of a loved one. Some of the most lasting conversions are of people who confessed a belief in the Lord following a funeral. As a preacher, some of the best sermons I've preached have been eulogies. God has a way of connecting us with the people who love him, even in death. The testimony of a great finish is to accept the gifts death offers.

Jesus speaks not only to Mary but also to John. John represents the future and community. The agony of the cross is transformed into the making of a future shaped in community. **Mary helps us consider how a testimony of a great finish is accepting the future that community gives us.** Jesus understood that Mary's future beyond the crucifixion was in community.

Too many of us isolate in grief. We shut down and shut out people. No one creates a future beyond trauma alone. Trauma in isolation kills. It has been aptly noted that the "challenge for trauma is having a home for our emotions."[15] Trauma needs a safe space to be worked out. It is only in community that a future will be found. We need people to pull us through, and people who love the Lord are future-oriented.

I had to go to Africa to get my shout on this text. I mentioned earlier how holding our loved ones in spaces of pain and grief prevents them from getting to their next assignment. I'm in the text! The Bible says, "From that time on, he took her to his house." After John commits to Mary and Mary commits to the future of community, Jesus speaks again. And one of those words was, *"Into Your hands, I commit my spirit."*

Mary let Jesus go, and Jesus committed his spirit to God. Mary moved on, and Jesus moved up. Mary committed to the future of the church, and Jesus committed to being Lord of the church. He moved on to his next assignment, from crucified Savior to Resurrected Lord. She saw him die on the Cross, but she saw him again on the other side of the grave.

Someone needs to hear me on this: **when we release our loved ones from pain, we release them to their next assignment.** When Mary let Jesus go in death, she was able to experience him in life during his next assignment as the Resurrected Lord. HALLELUJAH! BLESS HIS NAME!

DISCUSSION QUESTIONS

1. What have you experienced as the result of some real life moment having a great start? Did it finish well? If not, why not.

2. How have you handled life experiences that started well, but ended bad?

3. Name some grief in your life, or the life of your family, church, or community that has never been resolved.

4. Spend a moment considering what gifts have the loss of a loved one given to you.

5. What community held you and offered you a future beyond the pain of your loss? Did you receive it?

6. Is there some loss in your life that you are holding on to and preventing your loved one from moving on to his or her next assignment?

7. What consolation are you gaining from staying in pain?

8. Have you given thought on what resolution from your grief look like? If not, why not?

---

15 Kessler, David, Finding. Meaning: The Sixth Stage of Grief, (2019) Scribner Books of Simon and Shuster, p. 3.

A Word to the Reader

As you close this book, we invite you to do what we did at Bethlehem Missionary Baptist Church: listen again to Mary. Hear her voice not as a relic of the past but as a living testimony for the present. Let her sayings disrupt your complacency, enlarge your heart, call you to obedience, and teach you how to endure with resilience. And above all, let her words remind you that God is still breaking into the world through the voices of the silenced, the marginalized, and the overlooked.

Mary found us in Bethlehem. May she find you, too.

Live Hopeful,
Alvin & Diana

References

American Bible Society. (2000). *The Holy Bible: New Revised Standard Version.*

Archer, S. L. (2021). *Identity development: Adolescence through adulthood.* Sage Publications.

Baptist, E. E. (2014). *The half has never been told: Slavery and the making of American capitalism.* Basic Books.

Bernstine, A. C. (2023). *Preaching sermons that matter: A workbook on the dialectical model as taught by Samuel Dewitt Proctor.* BMBC Press.

Cleage, Albert B., Jr. (1968) *The Black Messiah: On Black Consciousness and Black Power*

Sheed and Ward Cone, J. H. (1970). *A Black theology of liberation.* J. B. Lippincott.

Erikson, S. (2020). *Honest Advent: Awakening to the wonder of God-with-us then, here, and now.* Zondervan.

Foster, F. S. (2018). *Written by herself: Literary production by African American women, 1746–1892.* Indiana University Press.

Gutiérrez, G. (1973). *A theology of liberation: History, politics, and salvation* (C. Inda & J. Eagleson, Trans.). Orbis Books. (Original work published 1971)

Johnson, J. W. (1926). *The book of American Negro spirituals.* Viking Press.

Jones, J. M., Hancock, S. S., & Shields, M. P. (2001). *The Black experience: Psychological, educational, and social perspectives.* Greenwood Publishing Group.

Kessler, David, Finding. Meaning: The Sixth Stage of Grief ( ), (2019)Scribner Books of Simon and Shuster.

McGrath, A. E. (2011). *Christian theology: An introduction* (5th ed.). Wiley-Blackwell.

Menakem, R. (2021). *My grandmother's hands: Racialized trauma and the pathway to mending our hearts and bodies.* Penguin Books.

Mauro, R. (2024). *The politics of redemption: Rethinking trauma and resistance.* Beacon Press.

Mitchell, Stephanie Y., (2002). Introducing Womanist Theology, Orbis Books.

Murro, M. (2020). *Unshackled: A story of resistance and restoration.* Chicago Review Press.

Nagel, T. (2020). *The view from nowhere.* Oxford University Press.

Nzegwu, N. (2011). Family matters: Feminist concepts in African philosophy of culture. In A. Oyěwùmí (Ed.), *African gender studies: A reader* (pp. 249–275). Palgrave Macmillan.

Perry, I. (2018). *Vexy thing: On gender and liberation*. Duke University Press.

Pierce, Y. (2021). *In my grandmother's house: Black women, faith, and the stories we inherit*. Broadleaf Books.

Richards, J. W., & O'Brien, D. J. (2012). *The American Catholic revolution: How the Sixties changed the church forever*. Oxford University Press.

Smith, M. J. (2022). *Toward a womanist ethic of incarnation: Black bodies, the Black church, and the council of Chalcedon*. Palgrave Macmillan.

Solomon, A. (2017). *Far from the tree: Parents, children and the search for identity*. Scribner.

Somé, M. P. (1997). *The spirit of intimacy: Ancient African teachings in the ways of relationships*. HarperOne.

St. Claire, R. (2007). In B. D. W. Smith, T. B. Dozeman, & C. L. West (Eds.), *True to our native land: An African American New Testament commentary* (pp. xxx–xxx). Fortress Press.

The Apostles' Creed. (n.d.). In *The Book of Common Prayer*. Episcopal Church.

Townes, E. M. (1995). *In a blaze of glory: Womanist spirituality as social witness*. Abingdon Press.

Williams, D. S. (1993). *Sisters in the wilderness: The challenge of womanist God-talk*. Orbis Books.

Williams, Theron (2022). Black Church, White Theology: How White Evangelicals Control the Black Church. Church Digest Books.

Work, M. (1940). *Negro folk songs*. University of North Carolina Press.

www.ingramcontent.com/pod-product-compliance
Lightning Source LLC
Chambersburg PA
CBHW080822120626
46556CB00010B/3361